The
Freedom
of a
Christian

The Freedom of a Christian

Grace, Vocation,
and the Meaning of Our
Humanity

Gilbert Meilaender

BrazosPress
Grand Rapids, Michigan

© 2006 by Gilbert Meilaender

Published by Brazos Press
a division of Baker Publishing Group
P.O. Box 6287, Grand Rapids, MI 49516-6287
www.brazospress.com

Printed in the United States of America

Library of Congress Cataloging-in-Publication Data
Meilaender, Gilbert, 1946–
       The Freedom of a Christian : grace, vocation, and the meaning of our humanity /
    Gilbert Meilaender.
          p.   cm.
    Includes bibliographical references.
    ISBN 10: 1-58743-193-9 (pbk.)
    ISBN 978-1-58743-193-7 (pbk.)
       1. Christian ethics. 2. Bioethics—Religious aspects—Christianity. 3. Christian
    ethics—Lutheran Church—Missouri Synod authors. I. Title.
    BJ1251.M43 2006
    241′.0441—dc22   2006005950

To Judy

whose vocation has been grace to me

Contents

Preface

Gathered in this volume are essays which, though about quite different topics, all deal with the shape of the Christian life as a life marked by freedom for hearing and obeying the command of God. The essays begin with three that take up the meaning of freedom largely as a theological problem, move through three that emphasize the way in which the call of God both frees and claims us, and end with five that consider how we may best preserve our humanity while living through a biotechnological revolution that often pictures human beings as nothing but the freedom to make and remake themselves.

It is, of course, somewhat with tongue in cheek that I have titled this volume *The Freedom of a Christian*—borrowing thereby the title of one of Martin Luther's most famous treatises (and, I might add, a treatise often misunderstood and misread). I have borrowed its title, however, because Lutheranism may be the branch of Christian tradition that has most often seemed to understand freedom in ways that leave no place for what Karl Barth called a "formed reference" to events.

Hence, the three essays in Part One focus closely on this theological problem and draw extensively on Lutheran resources—though just as much, in some respects, on Roman Catholic resources. After all, however much some contemporary Lutherans have attempted to think of Lutheranism as a free-standing theological system, it can really be understood only as

9

a correction within the Catholic tradition. It degenerates rapidly whenever its theologians attempt to build an entire system of Christian thought on ideas thought to be characteristically Lutheran (e.g., law/gospel, justification, paradox).

I prefer to think of the problem taken up by the three essays in Part One not as an idiosyncratically Lutheran one, but, rather, as a problem that is bound to arise in any system of Christian thought, one which it has sometimes been the burden of Lutheranism to raise. That problem can be stated in a number of ways, but perhaps most simply it is this: If the gospel announces that sinners are pardoned and that God is pleased with them, what more could possibly need doing? Why should we talk about these pardoned believers needing to learn to follow Christ, to obey the command of God, or to grow in grace and virtue? This is not a Lutheran problem; it is a problem for any theology that takes divine grace seriously. Therefore, the essays in Part One attempt to reclaim the *obedience* of faith within a life of Christian freedom.

This does not mean, however, that the whole of life becomes a matter of duty or obligation. In order to demonstrate and develop this, the essays in Part Two rework some themes that center on the idea of "vocation." This idea has also had considerable prominence in Lutheran theology, but I think any reader of these three essays will see that I am far from circling the wagons around a traditional understanding of it. For large stretches of life, vocation becomes permission to determine the person we will be, and even our duties are transformed when they become not just duties but the claim and command of God. More important still, perhaps, there is no limit given in advance to the divine summons. Hence, from one angle the calling sets us free; from another it utterly binds us. From one angle the calling directs us to a specific task; from another it sets us on an endless journey.

If we begin to understand our freedom within the contours sketched in Parts One and Two, we will be ready to think about the sorts of problems taken up in Part Three—and to do so without supposing that our human nature has no structure, that it is nothing other than the freedom to create and re-create ourselves. Ethical reflection, even when it takes Christian freedom seriously, ought to be able to give some "formed reference," some guidance about how we ought to live. Ethics that never does this scarcely deserves the name. Still, my aim in Part Three is not just to give guidance about what to do; it is, at least as much if not more, to think about biotechnological problems within the context of a Christian theology that—because it is free to talk about more than freedom—can discern something about the meaning of our humanity.

All of these essays have appeared elsewhere in print before. Some of them I have revised extensively, others more lightly. Some appeared in venues where footnotes were neither desired nor desirable, and I have not attempted here to supply them or alter their style. In his (characteristically brash) "Open Letter" dedicating "The Freedom of a Christian" to Pope Leo X, Luther wrote: "It is a small book if you regard its size. Unless I am mistaken, however, it contains the whole of Christian life in a brief form. . . ." Not even with tongue in cheek could I say that of the essays gathered here. I would say, however, that they take up themes very near the heart of Christian faith and life, and, in seeking to unpack the meaning of freedom, they explore a notion which many in our time have come to regard as the only truth about who and what we are. As will be apparent, that is a train I have no intention of boarding, for I do not think it can capture the freedom of those who have been claimed and called by God.

PART ONE

Freedom
for the Obedience
of Faith

1

Person and Work
in *Veritatis Splendor*[1]

W hen in August 1993, Pope John Paul II issued *Veritatis Splendor*, it was, according to the encyclical's own words, "the first time . . . that the Magisterium of the Church ha[d] set forth in detail the fundamental elements of this teaching."[2] The letter is divided into three chapters: the first offers a meditation on the story in Matthew's Gospel of the rich young ruler who comes to Jesus asking what he must do to be saved; the second treats controverted topics in moral theory (especially natural law and conscience, the meaning of a "fundamental option," and the concept of an intrinsically evil act); the third calls Christians to sacrifice even to the point of martyrdom in the service of moral truth and asserts the need for moral theologians to conform their teaching to that of the church.

Responses to the encyclical from Roman Catholic moral theologians generally praised the first chapter as an illustration of a renewed biblical spirituality in Catholicism and an example of John Paul's own serious reflection on the scriptures, but they were less generous—and sometimes harshly critical—with respect to the discussion of moral theory in chapter 2 or the "service" of moral theologians in chapter 3.[3]

Here I offer a different angle on the encyclical's teaching, an angle that will reopen some questions that perhaps first came to seem urgent at the time of the Reformation and played a role in the most significant split in the history of the Western church. These questions involve contrasting (and perhaps—but only perhaps—complementary) visions of the Christian life. If my reading of *Veritatis Splendor* is correct, they may still constitute an unresolved issue at the heart of Christian ethics, and an agenda for continuing work. From my angle of vision—focusing on the place of faith in the Christian life—it will turn out that chapter 1 of the encyclical is every bit as much cause for concern as chapter 2. Indeed, the supposed gap between them is not terribly important, for they are of a piece in ways central to my analysis.

In the encyclical's introduction John Paul expresses concern about a "frequently heard" opinion "which questions the intrinsic and unbreakable bond between faith and morality, as if membership in the Church and her internal unity were to be decided on the basis of faith alone while in the sphere of morality a pluralism of opinions and of kinds of behavior could be tolerated" (#4). Surely anyone drawn to the questions of the Reformation might perk up at such a sentence. Again, near the close of the encyclical's first chapter, John Paul writes: "No damage must be done to the *harmony between faith and life*" (#26). The relation between "faith and morals" was an important element in the Council of Trent's reaction to Lutheran teaching, and it is not the sort of problem one easily "resolves."[4] As our way into this issue I will focus on the encyclical's discussion of the story of the rich young ruler and its treatment of the notion of "fundamental option."

I

The first chapter of *Veritatis Splendor* is, even as biblical exposition, a tightly knit description of the moral life.[5] The young man comes to Jesus asking about the *telos* of life, the good he should seek. This is, ultimately, a question about God. But his question about the good turns out to be directly related to that other important moral concept, the right. To be directed toward God, as the man is by Jesus, is to be pointed toward the One who teaches us—through the natural law, the history of Israel, and the new covenant written on the heart—what is right to do. Teleology and deontology are in themselves insufficient, however. Both must be set into the context of the hope of eschatological perfection. Hence, the young man is called out on a journey toward human fulfillment. "Jesus shows that the commandments must not be understood as a minimum limit not to be gone beyond, but rather as a path involving a moral and spiritual journey towards perfection" (#15). That journey involves following Christ, being empowered by the Holy Spirit (since the new law, according to Aquinas, is finally the personal presence of the Spirit), and being guided by the church, which carries the tradition of faith and life entrusted to it by Jesus.

The precise role of grace in making possible this journey demands our attention, however. *Veritatis Splendor* describes the moral life as a response to "the many gratuitous initiatives taken by God out of love for man" (#10). It affirms that human fulfillment of the law comes only as a gift from God (#11). Yet it appears to picture such fulfillment of the law as a necessary *condition* of fellowship with God. That fellowship comes at the end of a long journey toward perfection, a journey empowered by grace (itself characterized as "the New Law" [#23]). Grace is fundamentally a power that makes possible that keeping of the law which constitutes the way back to God. "This is a still uncertain and fragile journey as long as we are on earth, but it is one made possible by grace, which enables us to possess the full freedom of the children of God" (#18).

Hence, the gift of grace has the effect of increasing the demands of the law. When the disciples, taken aback by Jesus's words to the rich young man, ask who then can be saved, Jesus responds: "With men this is impossible, but with God all things are possible." Drawing on a tradition of thought that goes back at least to Augustine's claim that God does not command the

impossible,[6] *Veritatis Splendor* understands Jesus's answer to mean
that grace is a power making possible the completion of the
journey toward perfection. "Keeping God's law in particular
situations can be difficult, extremely difficult, but it is never
impossible" (#102). Indeed, if a redeemed person still sins, this
can only be due to his unwillingness "to avail himself of the grace
which flows from" Christ's redemptive act (#103).

The way back to God is, therefore, the way of growth and
progress in keeping the moral law. Jesus, "the new Moses" (#12),
tells the young man to keep the commandments. When he affirms that he has in fact done so, Jesus calls him to perfection
(in the famous "if you would be perfect . . ." passage).

Is grace necessary even to begin this journey toward God?
Or is it necessary only for the completion of it? *Veritatis Splendor*
states that "the young man's commitment to respect all the moral
demands of the commandments represents the absolutely essential ground in which the desire for perfection can take root
and mature" (#17). Jesus helps the young man, we are told,
"to grasp *the conditions for the moral growth of man* . . . the young
man, having observed all the commandments, shows that he
is incapable of taking the next step by himself alone. To do so
requires mature human freedom . . . and God's gift of grace"
(#17).

Even if these words are not (as they sound) semi-Pelagian,
one might worry about the use of the language of "conditions"
for salvation here. At several other places similar language is
used: "Jesus himself definitively confirms them [the commandments of the Decalogue] and proposes them to us as the way
and condition of salvation" (#12). Or again, much later: "Jesus,
in his reply, confirms the young man's conviction: the perfor-
mance of good acts, commanded by the One who 'alone is good,'
constitutes the indispensable condition of and path to eternal
blessedness" (#72). With the Reformation disputes in mind,
one may legitimately wonder whether it would not have been
better, even from John Paul's perspective, to say that keeping
the commandments is a *description* of being on the way toward
fellowship with God, not a *condition* of it. The language of "con-

ditions" in these contexts risks undercutting the centrality of grace in the journey toward God.

Thus, a reader of the first chapter of *Veritatis Splendor* may be uncertain whether grace empowers the journey back to God from start to finish, or whether it only builds upon and helps to complete our own attempts to keep the commandments—which attempts constitute a necessary starting point for grace. Whatever the uncertainty on this point, however, a reader of chapter 1 will surely know that grace is necessary for the perfection of our fellowship with God. But the reader will also have learned to think of this necessary grace almost entirely in one way: as a power, as "an effective means for obeying God's holy law" (#114). Grace is absolutely essential, but "[i]t is precisely through his acts that man attains perfection as man" (#71). Grace makes possible growth and progress in righteous deeds; that is the picture of the Christian life at work in *Veritatis Splendor*.

II

What, if anything, does such a depiction of the Christian life lack? Taking the long way round to an answer, we can approach this question by considering another and quite different reading of the story of the rich young ruler: a seventeen-page small-print excursus buried deep within a discussion of "The Command as the Claim of God" in volume 2/2 of Karl Barth's *Church Dogmatics*.[7]

Characteristically, Barth begins by emphasizing that the entire action takes place within the sphere of Jesus Christ. Even the rich man, who is disobedient, is within that sphere. Hence, Barth does not think of one who is outside Christ's rule coming to him, coming from outside to inside. Instead, he thinks of all people as inside that sphere—either in obedience or in disobedience. Although that characteristic Barthian claim is unlike anything in *Veritatis Splendor*, the initial moves in Barth's exposition are not unlike John Paul's. Barth underlines the close connection between the two love commands. Every bit as much as John Paul, he emphasizes that "it is not possible to love God without then loving one's neighbour" (p. 616). The rich man's mistake lies in supposing that he can somehow separate the two commands (thus, one might say, divorcing faith from morals). Jesus's threefold word to him (sell what you have, give to the poor, and follow me) is designed to help him see his mistake. Just as *Veritatis Splendor* interprets the story as, finally, a call to follow Jesus, so does Barth. "He [the rich man] has all possessions except the one—the fulness of Jesus. And this is what condemns him" (p. 623).

Suddenly, however, Barth takes up a feature of the story almost entirely ignored in *Veritatis Splendor*—the disciples, those who are "the obedient" in contrast to the disobedient rich man. Barth notes their astonishment at Jesus's command to sell, give, and follow. The disciples have, in a sense, done this; nevertheless, they are astonished, and rightly so. For they now see clearly the lure of all they have forsaken, they understand its power, and they see that they themselves always stand "on the edge of the abyss of disobedience" (p. 624). One might have supposed that the only thing left for the disciples was greater growth in the way of life they had chosen in following Jesus. In Barth's depiction of them, however, there is no place for the language of growth and progress. Instead, even as "the obedient," the disciples learn again "how great a step obedience involves, and that even when this step has been taken once, it has to be taken again and again in all its difficulty" (p. 624). Not growth, but a continual return to the starting point characterizes the way of discipleship.

How, then, shall we depict that starting point? In the face of the disciples' astonishment, Jesus tells them that what is impossible for us is possible for God—a statement Barth describes as "obviously the hinge on which the whole narrative turns" (p. 625). Is this a promise that God will not command the impossible? Or that God will surely empower us to do what he commands? Not for Barth. His is a quite different move.

> [T]he impossible became possible to them. To them? No, it was never possible to them. It was still possible only to God. But in the knowledge that what is possible only to God has

become possible *for* them, in this confidence, in this humility or boldness—we can now say simply in *faith*—they became obedient. They accepted it as true that Jesus was obedient for them. . . . They believed, i.e., they were pleased to have His ability attributed to them, to have their own inability covered over by His ability. . . . They undertook to live in the shade and shelter of His ability. . . . If they do not lack the one thing that is needful for the fulfillment of the divine command, it is certainly not because they themselves possess it and achieve it. It is only because it is there for them in Jesus. It is only because they are pleased to accept it by faith in him. (p. 626)

The language of faith provides Barth's starting point here. It is not, however, a starting point from which one grows and develops, no longer standing on the edge of the abyss of disobedience. Rather, it is the starting point to which one constantly returns, covering one's inability by undertaking to live within the shade and shelter of Jesus's ability—which means not so much listening to the Teacher as trusting the Savior.

The disciples are "the obedient," the rich man "the disobedient"; yet "they stand with him under the judgment which is passed upon all that is possible with men, [and] he on his side is united with them under the promise of that which is possible with God" (p. 626). Hence, even for the obedient, even for the disciples, the Christian faith is not simply a journey toward perfection, described in terms of growth and progress. Unlike the rich man, the disciples have left everything to follow Jesus. When they point Jesus's attention to this fact—to the seeming difference between the obedient and the disobedient in the story—the reader suddenly realizes that they have made no progress. They still look back in sorrow at what they have left behind. "But how, then, had they really left it? . . . If they are capable of this backward look, are they even a single step in advance of the rich man who went away sorrowful?" (p. 628).

Even in the disobedience of these obedient disciples, Jesus promises them that they will have their reward in the kingdom (a promise which must, therefore, also be directed to the rich man in his disobedience). Confronted by the clear anxiety of his disciples, "[i]n face of their scarcely concealed defection,

Jesus becomes again and is again, and this time truly, Jesus the
Saviour" (p. 629). Not a Teacher, not a new Moses, not a living
and personal Law, not one to be imitated—not any of those roles
which chapter 1 of *Veritatis Splendor* ascribes to Jesus. With no
clear distinction remaining between the obedient and the disobedient, with both constantly standing on the edge of an abyss
they cannot cross, Jesus can only be the one who is *for* both. "He
steps, as it were, over that abyss for them and with them—again
making them, from what they are by themselves, into what they
are permitted to be by and with Him" (p. 629).

For *and* with them. They must therefore also step across that
abyss themselves to be with Jesus. They must grow in their discipleship. All that is true and present in Barth's exposition, yet
also somewhat muted. For in any moment "the obedient" may
suddenly realize the depth of their disobedience, may doubt
that any progress along the way of obedience has been made
in their life. At such moments—which means, potentially, at
any moment—they need to hear a promise they can trust, an
invitation not to moral struggle but to take shade and shelter
in the cover of Jesus's ability.

Structurally, Barth's exposition differs from John Paul's in that
it focuses not just on the rich man but also on the disciples—not
just the disobedient, but also the obedient. If, however, we ask
ourselves whether this structural difference has any theological
payoff, the answer is clear: It opens up space in Barth's exposition for the language of faith—language that, we may suddenly
realize, is virtually absent from chapter 1 of *Veritatis Splendor*.
It appears a few times in the sense of the "deposit of faith" or
in the phrase "faith and morals," but one must look hard to
find faith as *fiducia*. Perhaps we are close in a passage in which
faith is described as "even now . . . an inchoate share in the full
following of Christ" (#12). Closer still is paragraph 21, where
discipleship is described as becoming conformed to Christ,
who "dwells by faith in the heart of the believer." Closest of
all probably is the description in paragraph 19 of the response
of faith as something more than hearing a teaching or obeying
a commandment. "More radically, it involves *holding fast to the*

very person of Jesus, partaking of his life and his destiny, sharing
in his free and loving obedience to the will of the Father."

Does this relative lack of attention to faith as *fiducia* matter?
I do not wish to underestimate the importance of John Paul's
picture of the Christian life as a journey (empowered by grace)
toward perfection, nor the seriousness with which his invocation
of the church's martyrs reckons with the fact that this journey
may be difficult. At least in my view, no Christian ethic can get
along without these themes.[8] Nevertheless, taken alone, as they
for the most part are in *Veritatis Splendor,* they offer the *power* of
grace apart from its *pardon*—a grace that does not invite us in
our weakness simply to take shade and shelter in the fact that
Jesus is *for* us.

"It is precisely through his acts [empowered, to be sure, by
grace] that man attains perfection as man" (#71). Difficult to
encompass, however, within the categories of *Veritatis Splendor*
is the existential possibility that I might in my actions be disobedient and journeying away from the perfection God desires
of me while, simultaneously, through faith taking shelter in
Jesus as One whose acts of obedience have been done on my
behalf. Yet such a promise of shelter is the word of the gospel
as pardon, and the structure of what we say about the relation
of faith and morals should not undercut our ability to speak
that word of pardon when it is needed.

III

How diminished the significance of faith as *fiducia* is within
Veritatis Splendor will become clearer if we consider the treatment of fundamental option in its second chapter. This concept,
with its roots in transcendental Thomism, no doubt differs in
some respects from the Reformation language of faith, but it
also bears many similarities. In fact, *Veritatis Splendor* describes
the "decision of faith" as "a fundamental choice which qualifies
the moral life and engages freedom on a radical level before
God" (#66).

John Paul's concern is not so much with the concept itself as with the uses to which it can be put. He and those whom he criticizes agree, I think, in discerning a kind of two-way movement between particular acts and fundamental option. Particular actions can shape the fundamental orientation of the self, and that orientation is itself expressed in particular actions. In the categories of the Reformation, works can shape the person and the person is manifested in the works. At issue, though, is how tight the connection between these two must be. John Paul emphasizes that a fundamental choice for God cannot coexist with a deliberate choice to do what one knows to be gravely wrong.

Related to this issue, of course, is the debate about the category of intrinsically evil acts, a debate that I will not attempt to unravel here. In my judgment John Paul is correct to think that there may be some acts that are intrinsically evil, and he is right to view proportionalism as the practical equivalent of consequentialism, but these matters need not be resolved in order to get at my concerns. We need only note that John Paul thinks it impossible for a person to sustain a fundamental choice for God while knowingly and deliberately doing what is gravely wrong. He will allow no separation between judgment of the person and of the work. It may be that some of his critics agree with him on this point. Proportionalists' desire to demonstrate that they are not allowing the choice of moral evil (even though they may permit a choice of *pre*moral evil) suggests that they, too, may worry that deliberate evildoing is incompatible with a fundamental choice for God. In that case they remain essentially within John Paul's thought pattern (deliberate choice of grave evil must separate one from God), differing only on the question of whether at least some such choices can be specified as "intrinsically evil" in advance of any and all circumstances. If, however, one says with Josef Fuchs that "specific, individual moral acts as such are not the acceptance or rejection of grace," one may have adopted a different pattern of thought and set foot on a road that leads to Wittenberg.[9]

Discussing the place of norms within the Protestant tradition, Gene Outka has distinguished two questions:

(1) Does the violation of certain moral norms always negatively affect *one's own* relation to God? Does it necessarily influence, for example, one's prospects for salvation, or define in part the content of one's disobedience to God? (2) Does such violation always conflict with the normative content of *neighbor-love?* Are there certain actions one must never do to others if one genuinely loves them?[10]

Outka suggests that the Reformers tended to answer "no" to the first question, holding that our actions could not by themselves have decisive soteriological significance. Therefore, from this Reformation perspective, whether there are norms defining intrinsically evil acts will depend chiefly upon our answer to the second question. "Agent-performance loses some of its religious urgency and force; recipient-benefit becomes the primary criterion for making moral judgments."[11] If there are intrinsically evil acts, they are so because they could never, under any circumstances, be done as an expression of neighbor-love. Outka's distinction offers a useful angle from which to examine *Veritatis Splendor*.

In the encyclical intrinsically evil acts are evil for two reasons that are connected to the dual love command. First, they are evil because they violate the human dignity of the neighbor. "The different commandments of the Decalogue are really only so many reflections of the one commandment about the good of the person, at the level of the many different goods which characterize his identity as a spiritual and bodily being in relationship with God, with his neighbor and with the material world" (#13). But, second, intrinsically evil acts are also evil because they "are not capable of being ordered to God" (#81). Such *deeds*, at least if they involve grave matter, could be undertaken deliberately and knowingly only by a *person* who, by virtue of a fundamental choice, had turned against God.

When I agreed above that there may be intrinsically evil acts, I meant the first of these: that we may be able to specify in advance—apart, that is, from any particular circumstances—actions that would violate the neighbor's dignity. The question of fundamental option remains even after one has granted that.

Could such acts involving grave matter, undertaken knowingly and deliberately, be the acts of one who still had saving faith, who continued to take shade and shelter in the obedience of Jesus? Could the deed be intentionally sinful and the person right with God through faith? If that is possible, the connection between particular actions and fundamental option cannot be as tight as John Paul says it is. He explicitly considers a view for which the connection is not tight.

> According to the logic of the positions mentioned above, an individual could, by virtue of a fundamental option, remain faithful to God independently of whether or not certain of his choices and his acts are in conformity with specific moral norms or rules. By virtue of a primordial option for charity, that individual could continue to be morally good, persevere in God's grace and attain salvation, even if certain of his specific kinds of behavior were deliberately and gravely contrary to God's commandments as set forth by the Church (#68).

Such a position he rejects.

Human beings do not, John Paul says, "suffer perdition" only by a fundamental choice against God. On the contrary, with every deliberate and knowing choice of grave evil, one rejects God. There is no room for a divided self who chooses what is evil yet clings to God. Indeed, in what from a Reformation perspective is the most striking language in the encyclical, John Paul writes of one who freely commits mortal sin: "[E]ven if he perseveres in faith, he loses 'sanctifying grace,' 'charity' and 'eternal happiness.' As the Council of Trent teaches, 'the grace of justification once received is lost not only by apostasy, by which faith itself is lost, but also by any other mortal sin" (#68). If faith here means simply the "deposit of faith," a set of truths intellectually affirmed, it does not begin to capture the meaning of *fiducia*. If it means something more than that, if it includes the trust of the heart, then it is inconceivable that one persevering in such faith could lose eternal happiness.

At stake here, of course, is the meaning of the phrase *simul justus et peccator*, and I do not wish to overstate my claim. That any deliberate, knowing choice of evil may, in fact, enact a rejection of God and a refusal to trust I can hardly deny. That is what Helmut Thielicke meant by describing prohibited acts, *prohibitiva*, as "conditions under which, in principle, the work of the Holy Spirit cannot take place."[12] In such circumstances, Thielicke writes, in a striking sentence, "there is . . . no *simul*."[13]

But it is one thing to know that an act is evil in the sense that it always violates the dignity of one's neighbor. It is quite another to know that the evil of any act so overcomes the division of the self that there is no longer any *simul*, no longer a "disobedient" one who yet clings to the promise that in Jesus God is for us. Choosing to do what is gravely wrong, one might, of course, deliberately intend to reject the claims of any objective good outside the self—intend, that is, to reject God. One might also, however, while deliberately and knowingly choosing evil, say, "I know this is wrong, but it is the best I can manage here and now"—deliberately choosing *under the rubric of the good* what one knows to be wrong. If this is existentially possible, as I think it is, the *simul* is not necessarily destroyed in such a moment. The "disobedient" one clings to the promise, and we cannot deny that the promise is directed to him in all his disobedience.

Have I perhaps now pressed the Reformation position too far, driven too deep a wedge between judgment of the person and of the work? David Yeago has noted that Luther's understanding of the *simul* did not mean that no transformation of the sinner had taken place—as if we could be "unchanged but accepted." Rather, it meant that the remaining sin which clings to a believer is sin that does not "rule" the believer's action. "The sin in question is located 'within' in the heart, not 'without in the believer's walk.'" Serious examples of such remaining sin are Peter's denial and David's adultery and murder. These "do not negate their identity as believers" because, on the one hand, these sins "were not entered with full deliberateness," and, on the other, "were *repented of* as soon as the one who committed them became aware of what he had done." Hence, "deliberate *peccatum actuale* is not really compatible with faith in Christ *at all*."[14]

One could support Yeago's claim with passages from the Lutheran Reformers. Thus, for example, in his 1555 *Loci Communes*, Melanchthon argues that we must make a distinction between different kinds of sin.[15] Although his distinction is similar to the Roman Catholic distinction between mortal and venial sin, it does not depend on any judgment of the *gravity* of the sin. Rather, *deliberateness* is the key. Granting that sin still clings to the saints in this life—and that it is truly sin—he nonetheless distinguishes between instances in which "a man acts against his conscience, that is, consciously and willingly against the command of God" and instances which "are not sins against conscience." The latter, although not insignificant, do not blot out the holiness of the believer "as long as we do not will to follow these evil tendencies with action, but painfully strive against them." But those "who consciously follow their evil tendencies with action . . . and those who are not converted again fall into eternal punishment."

Perhaps even more important, similar assumptions can be detected at work in several of the Lutheran Confessional writings. Thus, for example, the *Epitome* of the *Formula of Concord*, while maintaining that the good works which follow faith are not the ground of our justification before God, notes (3.11): "Nevertheless, we should not imagine a kind of faith in this connection that could coexist and co-persist with a wicked intention to sin and to act contrary to one's conscience. On the contrary, after a person has been justified by faith, a true living faith becomes 'active through love' (Gal. 5:6)." Even more striking, perhaps, the *Smalcald Articles*, authored by Luther himself, state (3.3.43–44): "It is therefore necessary to know and to teach that when holy people, aside from the fact that they still possess and feel original sin and daily repent and strive against it, fall into open sin (as David fell into adultery, murder, and blasphemy), faith and the Spirit have departed from them. This is so because the Holy Spirit does not permit sin to rule and gain the upper hand in such a way that sin is committed, but the Holy Spirit represses and restrains it so that it does not do what it wishes. If sin does what it wishes, the Holy Spirit and faith are not present."

That these questions are neither straightforward nor un-complicated may be seen, however, if we take note of a similar passage in Luther's 1535 Galatians commentary. Discussing Galatians 5:19, he writes:

> Nevertheless, it sometimes happens that the saints may lapse and gratify the desires of their flesh. Thus David, in a great and horrible lapse, fell into adultery and was responsible for the murder of many when he had Uriah die in battle (2 Sam. 11). . . . Peter also lapsed horribly when he denied Christ. But no matter how great these sins were, they were not committed intentionally; they were committed because of weakness. In addition, when they had been admonished, these men did not persist stubbornly in their sins but returned to their senses. . . . Those who sin because of weakness, even if they do it often, will not be denied forgiveness, provided that they rise again and do not persist in their sins; for persistence in sin is the worst of all. If they do not return to their senses but stubbornly go on gratifying the desires of their flesh, this is the surest possible sign of dishonesty in their spirit. . . . Anyone who yields to his flesh and persists in smugly gratifying its desires should know that he does not belong to Christ.[16]

In the passage cited earlier from the *Smalcald Articles,* Luther treats David's sin not simply as a sin of weakness into which a saint might fall, but as intentional sin that is incompatible with faith and the presence of the Holy Spirit. Here in the Galatians commentary he treats it as a sin of weakness that is not committed intentionally and that, presumably, does not involve the kind of smug persistence in sin that makes it impossible for one simultaneously to belong to Christ. This ought to warn us that even if deliberate choice of evil involves rejection of God, as may surely sometimes be true, these cases are not easy to parse.

The human psyche is too complicated and the human will too deeply divided to admit of any general rule here. Clearly, one who deliberately does what he believes to be wrong steps into dangerous territory, for he goes against conscience. But can one who does this out of a deeply divided self, unable to will undividedly what he knows to be right, properly be described

as one who persists in "smugly gratifying" the desires of the
flesh? Should we be certain that, even in such a person, God's
healing grace is powerless and without effect? Or that such a
one, even in his disobedience, is not also seeking to live under
the shade and shelter of God's grace?

To suggest, as I have, that deliberate intention to commit
grave sin may sometimes coexist with saving faith is not a claim
upon which to build an ethic. Whatever we conclude about the
possible coexistence of *fiducia* with a deliberate intention to do
wrong, it is still an intention *to do wrong*. Wrongs done by the
believer are covered by the righteousness of Christ; they are
not thereby made right. And to the degree that John Paul has
in *Veritatis Splendor* trained his sights upon any who, in effect,
claim that the subjective good of a fundamental choice for God
overcomes the objective wrongness of a sinful act, he is certainly
on target. Such a view loses the distinction between judgment of
the person and of the work by folding the latter into the former.
That would be no better—indeed, perhaps worse—than John
Paul's own tendency to make judgment of the work determinative for judgment of the person. Two fundamentally different
judgments are involved here, and neither can be collapsed into
the other prior to that eschatological judgment in which the
truth of each person will be revealed. In the meantime, however,
the life of faith is precisely that in which we struggle to believe
about ourselves what is not always manifest in our desires, our
wills, and, even our choices and actions—namely, that we belong
to the Spirit of Christ and are therefore, in God's eyes, wholly
and entirely righteous.

In taking up the possibility of deliberate wrongdoing by a
believer, we are not, therefore, constructing an ethic. We are
situating ourselves to practice that most difficult of theological
arts—the distinction of law and gospel—in the care of souls.
To one whom we judge to be smugly persisting in sin, one
kind of response is necessary. To another whom we judge to
be clinging to Christ even in his sin, another kind of response is
needed. No general rule can be given here, for the art of theological judgment is needed. We should not, I repeat, attempt
to spin an ethic out of the distinction between law and gospel,

but neither should we imagine that the care of souls can be satisfactorily carried out unless and until we have loosened the tight fit that John Paul has established between judgments of the work and of the person.[17]

That this is not a problem for Christian theology alone is nicely illustrated by Jonathan Sacks, Chief Rabbi of Great Britain. Sacks discusses the problem Moroccan Jews faced in the twelfth century when political power was seized by a Muslim sect that undertook a policy of forced conversions to Islam.[18] Some Jews chose to become martyrs, but, of course, others did not have within themselves the stuff of the martyr. Many of these "conversos" or "marranos" publicly embraced Islam "though inwardly remaining Jews and practicing Judaism in secret." How were they to be judged? Some rabbis held that they were "no longer part of the house of Israel." Maimonides, however, in his "Epistle on Forced Conversion," argued otherwise. What Sacks finds so instructive in Maimonides' argument, however, and what is so appropriate to my concern here, is that Maimonides was uncompromising in his judgment that the conversos had acted wrongly. Yet they were not excluded from the house of Israel. "There is nothing equivocal about Maimonides' defense of those who yielded to presssure. Nor is there any ambivalence about his later analysis of what, in fact, is the right way to behave. He invests both with equal seriousness." That is, he recognizes that there can be no perfect fit between judgment of the person and judgment of the work.

Distinguishing these two judgments always opens up the possibility of abuse, of course, and that is to some degree the worry of John Paul in *Veritatis Splendor*. We should take the danger seriously, but I know of no solution to it other than a determined commitment to make both sorts of judgments whenever they are necessary.

In his *Theology of the Lutheran Confessions* Edmund Schlink devotes two chapters to the distinction between law and gospel.[19] First he follows a way that leads from law to gospel. That is, consciousness of the law's condemnation drives us along the way that leads to the gospel's promise. But there is also a way that leads from gospel to law. The announcement of the gospel's power to renew our lives may become a condemning word (law) for us; for, if we do not seem to experience transformation or new obedience, we may come to doubt our renewal. "If faith cannot coexist with sin, with sinful desires, or with the intention to sin, whose faith is then still faith?"[20] That is, the truth that sin no longer rules in the life of the regenerate, since they are no longer *under* the law, can in some moments of weakness lead us to doubt whether we have the Spirit of Christ.

The difficulty should by now be clear: On the one hand, we must never construct an ethic that makes it impossible for us both to condemn (when appropriate) and to comfort (when appropriate) the consciences of those for whom we are responsible. Hence, we should not permit our judgment of the person simply to determine our judgment of the work—as if a believer should never be warned that his action endangers his continued membership in Christ's Body. At the same time, we cannot state—as a general rule, in advance of the care of any particular individual—that an objectively wrong deed, even a gravely wrong deed, cannot coexist with saving faith. We must strive to retain the capacity to make each judgment—of the work and of the person—as it is needed.

There is no easier or less complicated way to capture the full significance of the fact that in this life the Christian remains *simul justus et peccator*. That formula must always be taken in two somewhat different ways; for God's grace in Christ is both transforming power and declaration of pardon. As transforming power it enters into the history of our lives, driving out the sin that still clings, drawing us ever more fully into the holiness of Christ, making possible continued growth in righteousness, giving a direction to the moral life, and fitting us for heaven. Yet, as Schlink noted, this very description of grace as transforming power can be heard not as pardon but as condemnation when we do not see in ourselves the signs of continued growth, when we turn away from the holiness to which Christ calls us. And when we turn away, drawn by the continuing lure of sin, we will need—at different times and in differing measures—not only a word warning us of our spiritual peril but also a word pardoning us precisely in our ungodliness (Rom. 5:6).

In 2 Kings the prophet Elisha heals Naaman, commander of the army of the king of Syria. In gratitude, Naaman tries, before returning home, to bestow gifts upon the prophet, but Elisha does not accept them.

> Then Naaman said, "If not, I pray you, let there be given to your servant two mules' burden of earth; for henceforth your servant will not offer burnt offering or sacrifice to any god but the LORD. In this matter may the LORD pardon your servant: when my master goes into the house of Rimmon to worship there, leaning on my arm, and I bow myself in the house of Rimmon, when I bow myself in the house of Rimmon, the LORD pardon your servant in this matter." He said to him, "Go in peace."[21]

Naaman does not yet seem to have in him the stuff of a martyr. Perhaps that later changed in his journey toward perfection. We are not told. But Naaman also does not, at least in this sparse account, claim that an appreciation of his circumstances will make what he does right. He simply asks for pardon. He stands therefore as an instance of the truth that, short of the eschatological perfection to which we are indeed called, judgment of the work and judgment of the person cannot perfectly coincide. He reminds us that, even as we should not construct a theological ethic that is unable to call his deed wrong, so also we should not construct an ethic that makes it impossible for us to say with Elisha: "Go in peace."

IV

I have attempted to reopen some Reformation questions and direct them to *Veritatis Splendor* in a way that other commentators have not, to my knowledge, done. It is important, therefore, to repeat what I said earlier: No Christian ethic can say everything that needs saying solely through the Reformation language of "faith active in love." If we dare never say for certain that a particular deed makes the *simul* of faith impossible, we ought not deny that our deeds do shape our character—and that they have the power to make of us people who no longer trust God for our security in life and in death. Nor ought we deny that the transforming power of grace works to heal the division within our will, so that sin no longer has us in its power.

But alongside that affirmation of the soul-making power of what we do must be placed an equally strong affirmation of God's promise of pardon to the disobedient *in* their disobedience—a pardon that must sometimes be trusted in the face of considerable evidence to the contrary in our lives. The Reformers emphasized not only *sola gratia* but also *sola fide*. If *Veritatis Splendor* grasps—albeit a bit haltingly in places—the importance of *sola gratia,* it fails to enunciate clearly the *sola fide.* It is necessary, therefore, to reassert beside its pattern of thought the centrality of the language of faith for Christian life.

If *Veritatis Splendor* requires such correction or supplement, it is at least also true that it speaks a theological language serious enough to invite such a response. One is—or, at least, I am— hard pressed to imagine an equally serious statement on the nature of theological ethics issuing at this time from any major Protestant body. Those who wish to keep alive the questions of the Reformation and the centrality of the language of faith in our vision of the Christian life must therefore be thankful for *Veritatis Splendor.*

Notes

1. Earlier, somewhat different versions of this chapter (as I keep trying to get it right!) have appeared as: (1) "*Veritatis Splendor*: Reopening Some Questions of the Reformation," *Journal of Religious Ethics,* 23 (Fall 1995), pp. 225–38; (2) "Grace, Justification through Faith, and Sin," pp. 60–83 in Reinhard Hütter and Theodor Dieter (eds.), *Ecumenical Ventures in Ethics* (Grand Rapids: Eerdmans, 1998).

2. Pope John Paul II, *The Splendor of Truth* (Boston: St. Paul Books & Media, 1993), #115. Citations of the encyclical will hereafter be identified by paragraph number in parentheses within the body of the text.

3. See, for example, Richard A. McCormick, S.J., "Some Early Reactions to *Veritatis Splendor,*" *Theological Studies,* 55 (September 1994), pp. 481–506. One gets a sense of how harsh the criticism could be when McCormick writes (p. 483) that the encyclical's "analyses [are] too frequently obscure and convoluted, and its presentation of revisionist tendencies [is] tendentious, extreme, and ultimately inaccurate."

4. John Mahoney, *The Making of Moral Theology* (Oxford: Clarendon Press, 1987), pp. 120–35.

5. I have drawn this description from the careful summary of Oliver O'Donovan, "A Summons to Reality," in *Understanding "Veritatis Splendor*," ed. John Wilkins (London: SPCK, 1994), pp. 41–42.

6. Cf. Mahoney, pp. 48–57.

7. Karl Barth, *Church Dogmatics II/2* (Edinburgh: T & T Clark, 1957), pp. 613–30. Citations will be given by page number in parentheses within the body of the text. Stanley Hauerwas noted this "fascinating parallel," but without considering it in detail. See his brief essay "*Veritatis Splendor*," *Commonweal*, 120 (October 22, 1993), p. 16.

8. Cf. Gilbert C. Meilaender, *The Theory and Practice of Virtue* (Notre Dame, IN: University of Notre Dame Press, 1984), pp. 100–26; Gibert C. Meilaender, *Faith and Faithfulness* (Notre Dame, IN: University of Notre Dame Press, 1991), pp. 74–80.

9. Josef Fuchs, "Basic Freedom and Morality," in Ronald P. Hamel and Kenneth R. Himes (ed.), *Introduction to Christian Ethics: A Reader* (Mahway, NJ: Paulist Press, 1989), p. 196.

10. Gene Outka, "The Protestant Tradition and Exceptionless Moral Norms," in Donald G. McCarthy (ed.), *Moral Theology Today: Certitudes and Doubts* (St. Louis: The Pope John Center, 1984), p. 137.

11. Ibid., p. 138.

12. Helmut Thielicke, *Theological Ethics*, Vol. 1 (Philadelphia: Fortress Press, 1966), p. 87.

13. Ibid., p. 89.

14. David Yeago, personal communication (December 4, 1995).

15. For the following, see Clyde L. Manschreck (ed.), *Melanchthon on Christian Doctrine* (New York: Oxford University Press, 1965), pp. 183–86.

16. *Luther's Works*, vol. 27 (St. Louis: Concordia Publishing House, 1964), pp. 80–81.

17. An instructive example of the difficulties Roman Catholic practice encounters here arises in the pastoral care of those who are divorced and remarried. To be sure, all honor should be given to the seriousness with which the Roman Church attempts to uphold Christian teaching concerning marriage. Protestants, who have for the most part lost all such seriousness, are in no position to cast stones. But the difficulties of maintaining that the divorced remarried continue to belong to the church but are excluded from the Eucharist are profound. For an instructive discussion both of the complexity and seriousness of Catholic thought on this question, and of its shortcomings, see Kenneth R. Himes O.F.M. and James A. Coriden, "Notes on Moral Theology 1995: Pastoral Care of the Divorced and Remarried," *Theological Studies*, 57 (March 1996), pp. 97–123.

18. Jonathan Sacks, "To Be a Prophet for the People," *First Things*, no. 59 (January 1996), pp. 27–29.

19. Edmund Schlink, *Theology of the Lutheran Confessions* (Philadelphia: Fortress Press, 1961). See chapters 3 and 4.

20. Ibid., p. 117.

21. 2 Kings 5:17–19.

2

―――⟶⟩⦿⟨⟵―――

Hearts Set to Obey[1]

At least since the seventh century, and no doubt even earlier, Christians have been praying, in the words of the Collect for Peace, used in Vespers: "O God, from whom come all holy desires, all good counsels, and all just works: Give to us, your servants, that peace which the world cannot give, that our hearts may be set to obey your commandments. . . ." Any theological system or construct that, in effect, subverts such a prayer or, even if only implicitly, suggests that we might be wrong to pray in this way, invites our attention. And we know that—of all the trajectories within the history of Christian thought—it is Lutheran theology that has perhaps most often been suspected of undercutting such a prayer. Not that Lutherans have ceased to pray it, of course. To that degree, perhaps, their practice has sometimes been better than their theory.

I aim to examine critically a certain understanding of Lutheranism, which (whether our language is that of paradox, of the law-gospel distinction, of the law as always accusing, of dialectic, or of freedom from law and critique of any third use of the law) eventually arrives at a kind of practical antinomianism—which is, alas, all too readily accompanied by a strident moralism—but which, were it consistent, would have no reason to pray that our hearts may be set to obey God's commandments.

It is important to observe at the outset, however, that the problem I examine is not simply a Lutheran problem. The tension between two understandings of the person—one whose self is shaped by what one does, or one whose deeds reflect the person one is (declared by God to be)—goes deep into the heart of the Christian tradition more generally.[2] It is fair to say, though, that this tension has been more pronounced at some places within the tradition, and Lutheranism has been such a place. Hence, it provides our point of entry here.

I

Whether we prefer the language of law, of command, or of evangelical imperative, our concern is to examine the place within Christian life of "the unchanging will of God, according to which human beings are to conduct themselves in this life," as the Formula of Concord defines the "one single meaning" of the word "law."[3] This will of God that is to structure the conduct of our lives is made known to us in several ways. The God of Abraham, Isaac, and Jacob binds himself to his people in covenant fidelity, and that covenant, in turn, calls for their responsible obedience. The will of the covenanting Lord is given to Israel in the commands of Sinai—which, in the simplest sense, call for avoidance of any idolatry and for structures of life that honor the neighbor and bind human lives together in community. The gift of the Sinai covenant is honored time and again by the great prophets of Israel, whose focal point is often Israel's failure to be faithful to her covenant obligations.

One encounters the will of God not only in the covenant but also in the structure of creation itself. The God who commands at Sinai has created a world with a morally coherent shape and form—a shape that is knowable, at least in part, also by those who have not yet bound themselves in covenant with Israel's

God. And, indeed, the wisdom traditions recorded in the Bible must be the fruit of long reflection on this moral form of the created order.

These two revelations of God's will—the commandments of Torah and the structure of creation—cohere, as is nicely illustrated, for example, in Psalm 19. The psalmist affirms that "[t]he heavens are telling the glory of God." Without speech or words in any ordinary sense, the creation does not confront us with the personal address of one who commands. Yet the firmament proclaims its Creator's handiwork in its coherent moral order which "day to day pours forth speech / and night to night declares knowledge." Israel's God does not, however, leave his people to their own inadequate attempts to discern this order embedded in the creation. He is gracious enough to speak, to command, as the psalmist also recognizes. "The law of the LORD is perfect, reviving the soul."[4] Not without good reason, therefore, does Bonhoeffer write, referring to this psalm and several others that make God's law the object of praise, "It is grace to know God's commands."[5]

We know, of course, that in the history of redemption the incarnate God himself must finally vindicate the moral order of creation in the face of human failure and disobedience. Moreover, we who in our baptism have come to name Jesus as Lord, are now called not just to discern the shape of creation or listen for the commands of Torah, but also to understand the moral life as discipleship, as following Jesus in his obedience to the Father. "Have this mind among yourselves, which you have in Christ Jesus," Paul writes in Philippians. Or, as the hymn puts it: "Let us ever walk with Jesus / Follow his example pure. . . . Let us do the Father's bidding."

Romans 6 sets the terms for our discipleship. As we seek daily to creep ever more fully into our baptism, we struggle to distinguish between those actions that follow Christ and those that do not. When we encounter the will of God in the moral order of creation or in the commands of Torah, we quickly realize that—because we have not yet come to the end of the history of redemption or to the end of our own personal way as followers of Jesus—the new life into which we are baptized must sometimes be believed more than seen. Hence, the note of eschatological reservation, the sense that we are only on the way, in Romans 6: "For if we have been united with him in a death like his, we shall certainly be united with him in a resurrection like his." We remain both sinner and saint as long as we are in this life, but ours is not a static condition. The grace of God enables us, along the way, to grow in the life of discipleship.

For something decisive has happened. "We were buried therefore with him by baptism into death, so that as Christ was raised from the dead by the glory of the Father, we too might walk in newness of life." We are no longer "enslaved" to sin. In Christ Jesus we are "alive to God"—desiring to know his will and learning to delight in his commands. And, although as followers on the way we sin daily, we are no longer in bondage to that sin. Something has happened. There is movement in this story that is the history of redemption. "For sin will have no dominion over you, since you are not under law but under grace." Our hearts are now set to obey the commandments of the God whose face we have seen in the crucified and risen One.

To be sure, it is also true that at any moment we may experience ourselves as caught between the continuing hold of sin and our liberation in Christ. We may experience our condition as both saint and sinner in a more static way. In those moments the history of redemption may seem to be less a story with movement and direction than a never-ending battle between the powerful grip of sin and the new life under grace into which we have been baptized. I would never wish to deny the importance of this recurring experience in the life of disciples. It is of enormous significance for pastoral care in ways, but it should not become the chief structuring principle of Christian ethics—as if the only issue for theology were to understand the indefinitely repeated, momentary *transition* from fallen to new creation, or as if the whole of our theological attention should be focused on those who find themselves in situations of extreme temptation and anxiety.[6] Rather, although theologians must be constantly alert to the possibility of such extremity of despair, they need not do their work under a kind of self-denying ordinance that forbids attention to anything other than the transition from sin to grace, from despair to faith.

How, then, should we respond in the face of that recurring experience of the power of sin? Part of the answer, of course, is that these are the moments in Christians' lives when the language of faith is a necessity: We *trust* that the grace of God in Christ has pardoned our sin and set us free for discipleship even in those moments when we cannot experience it happening. But there is still more to be said. We not only trust that God has done this—as if we could simply rest content in simultaneously experiencing our enslavement to sin and our trust in a pardoning God, as if we could simply salute the grace of God and go on our way. We not only trust; we also pray. We pray that, by the grace of God, the new life in Christ—the new thing that has happened, whether it is for the moment apparent or not—would, day by day, take an increasingly firm hold upon our hearts, that they might be set to obey God's commandments. It is in no way contrary to the life of discipleship that we should, again and again, experience ourselves as simply caught in the tension between the reality of our sin and the reality of God's forgiveness. What *is* contrary to the path of discipleship is that we should rest content in that static condition, that we should not in prayer strain against it as we ask Christ's Spirit to make the history of redemption an ever more effective reality in what we think, say, and do. "Strive," says the Letter to the Hebrews, "for the holiness without which no one will see the Lord."

II

I said at the outset that Lutheran theology has sometimes been suspected of undermining this striving for holiness—"[s]lackness is the hereditary sin of Lutheranism," as Einar Billing put it[7]— and we need now to examine more systematically why this has been the case. Certainly there are important strands in Luther's thought which, seeming to divorce theology from ethics and faith from life, might, as John Witte has noted, "lead an earnest Evangelical follower straight into antinomianism."[8] Of course, even were this true of everything that Luther wrote—as it is not—it would still be the case that Luther is not Lutheranism, and Witte's work makes clear how quickly Lutheran jurists in Germany began to fashion "reformation laws" that gave moral form and social shape to the life of their duly reformed cities. "When properly understood and applied," they believed, "the law not only coerced sinners, it also educated saints."[9]

What the jurists thought it necesary to do, and what they thought perfectly continuous with Luther's theology, others have viewed as a betrayal. Lutheranism can be depicted as having a kind of allergy to law, and the characteristically Lutheran distinction between law and gospel can be presented not as a corrective to abuses that had arisen within the church but, rather, as the basis for an entirely new system of theology. Instead of serving as a distinction important for pastoral care of believers who are "on the way" in the midst of the history of redemption, it can become, as David Yeago observes, "the prime structuring principle" of all Christian theology.[10] We should note, in passing, the peculiarity of this tendency. After all, the Lutheran Confessional writings begin with the ecumenical creeds, and the first three articles of the Augsburg Confession simply reaffirm received Christian teaching about the Triune God, about sin, and about Christ. This does not suggest an attempt to develop a theology structured in an entirely novel way. Peculiar or not, however, the claim of novelty is dear to the hearts of many Lutherans, and it therefore needs our examination.

One of the most straightforward developments of this view of Lutheranism—as a "dialectical" theology that separates theology from ethics—can be found in a recent book by Daphne Hampson, *Christian Contradictions: The Structures of Lutheran and Catholic Thought*.[11] Perhaps because she no longer regards herself as a Christian and thinks that the basic framework of Christian theology must be discarded in the modern age, Hampson is unusually free to think through the implications of a dialectical Lutheranism, which, though it does not persuade her, she has often found attractive.[12]

She contrasts Lutheranism's "dialectic" framework of thought with Catholicism's "linear" framework. For Catholicism, that is,

the Christian life is understood as a *via*, a journey (destined ultimately to end in the vision of God). At least at its non-Pelagian
best, Catholicism emphasized prevenient grace, understanding
it as the justifying power that made possible gradual progress
toward a holiness that was fit to stand before God. Hence, the
Catholic understanding of righteousness is substantive (a quality that inheres in the person) and quantitative (achieved bit by
bit, a matter of more and more). Our sinful nature is gradually
transformed and perfected along the way. One can even use
the characteristically Lutheran formula of *simul justus et peccator*, but in this framework the formula must be understood
quantitatively. Divine grace is a power that gradually makes us
"more and more" righteous—less sinner, more saint, to put
it a bit too crudely. "This way of thinking," Hampson writes,
"is to have far-reaching implications for the whole of Catholic
life. It will mean that all kinds of matters, whether euthanasia
or questions of sexual ethics, are of fundamental concern to the
church. By contrast, . . . for Protestants the world is a secular
sphere, in which humans make their own arrangements according to their own lights" (pp. 86f.). A more succinct—and
telling—characterization of where many Protestant churches
find themselves today would be hard to imagine.[13]

The dialectical framework of Lutheran theology, by contrast,
dispenses entirely, at least on Hampson's telling, with such
linear notions of gradual growth in righteousness. Indeed, "the
whole thrust of the Lutheran tradition is," she writes, "against
self-perfection" (p. 51). Stronger still, even if in some tension
with Jesus's words in Matthew 5:48, she writes: "The Christian
is free not to be perfect" (p. 287). We accept—perhaps, in subtle
ways, we even delight in—our condition as simultaneously saint
and sinner. The only righteousness of concern to the Christian
is extrinsic, the righteousness of Christ. Hence, the Lutheran
understanding of righteousness is relational (rather than being
a quality that inheres in a person). Grace is in no sense a power
that enables us to become "more and more" what God wills
we should be; rather, grace is pardon that announces God's
acceptance of the sinner and thereby elicits the faith that puts
sinners in right relation with God.

That grace having been announced, there is no more to be said—other than to say it "again and again."[14] That is, any serious struggle to grow in righteousness, to obey God's commands more fully, will be understood as sin, since it may direct one's attention inward in a self-preoccupied way, rather than outward to the extrinsic righteousness of Christ. From such self-perfecting tendencies one must simply flee again and again. Christians never grow in righteousness; they simply return time and again to the word that announces pardon, a word that invites and elicits faith. They continually reclaim their starting point.

It is hard to know exactly how one who lived solely within this framework of thought could raise children or pass on the church's way of life. There is room here for preaching, but perhaps not for catechesis. And there can be no place for ethical reflection or instruction. According to this dialectical framework, the church must strictly separate faith from life. It should confine itself to preaching the gospel that frees us from self-preoccupation. Again and again. If it talks of God's commandments, it does so in order to see how they condemn us and how we must—again and again—flee from that condemnation to the gospel's announcement of pardon.

In short, the central element in Hampson's analysis can be stated simply and clearly: For Luther or Lutheranism, righteousness is in no sense substantive; it is not a quality that—even by God's grace—inheres in believers. Hence, there is no sense in which righteousness can grow, in which the grace of God should be understood as a power that makes possible the Christian's journey toward holiness. On the contrary, righteousness is entirely a relation. To have faith in Christ is to have his righteousness and, therefore, to be right with God. What more could be needed? Having that, there is no need for growth. There is need only to return again and again to the promise that elicits faith in Christ as our righteousness. Christians are not on the way. The Christian life goes nowhere. Rather, it returns—again and again. It starts over. It is a constant return to the promise, a constant struggle to trust that Christ is indeed our righteousness. Moreover, serious attention to the moral life and to God's commands, serious ethical reflection about the sort

of acts we should do and the sort of persons we should be, must
be renounced as temptation. Expressing a sinful preoccupation
with self, such concern simply demonstrates that, in ourselves,
we are indeed wholly and entirely slaves to sin.

Before turning to more systematic examination of the ad-
equacy of this characterization of Lutheran theology, it may be
worth making a passing observation about the system of thought
Hampson depicts. This approach to theology—important for
pastoral care as it sometimes is—narrows our range of vision
considerably. We can put this point in terms used by Robert
Scharlemann in his comparative study of the theology of Aquinas
and Gerhard. The object of Gerhard's theological attention—in
characteristically dialectical fashion—"is not the whole picture
of man as he is by nature and by grace, but the picture of man
precisely at the point of transition between the two states."[15]
Consequently, what one should say theologically always depends
on the state of the person to whom one speaks, and there seem
to be only two such states that play a determinative role in a
dialectical theology: the person addressed is either "complacent
man" or "despairing man." If complacent, he must be brought
to despair; if despairing, he is ready to hear the gospel.

But are these the only two sorts of people whom we might
address? Are there none who, neither complacent nor despairing, are simply baptized Christians who know that they are no
longer in bondage to sin but are still sinners who need to grow in
grace? How ought one speak to them? Or must we tacitly assume
that they are really complacent and must be moved to despair
before we have anything else to say to them? A theology that
puts the language of "paradox" front and center, once we start
to press upon it, is likely to leave us with such questions.[16]

Having been more or less trained in such an approach to
Lutheran theology, I recall that I sensed there was something
wrong with it long before I began to be able to say what that
might be. I first thought that what was mistaken about this way
of structuring a theological system was that it lacked a doctrine
of creation. Unwilling to talk of a moral order embedded in the
creation, it seemed unable to say that our action should conform
to that order. I still think there is something to that first thought

of mine; that is, there are moments when an incipient Marcionite tendency makes its presence felt in this version of Lutheran theology. But I now wonder whether something almost the opposite might not come even closer to the truth, whether it might not be more accurate to say that this approach has *nothing but* a doctrine of creation.[17] It is just creation and new creation "again and again." Nothing else ever happens. There is no movement, no *history* of redemption. There is only the moment of transition from sin to faith, returned to time and again. No person whom God has created is set on the way toward progress in the new life—only created again and again.

III

Not without good reason, therefore, has Niels Henrik Gregersen argued that "Luther's dialectic of law and gospel should not be elevated into a theological principle that structures the interpretation of Christian faith from beginning to end." When that is done, Gregersen notes, we end with a theology that "cannot express the extent to which the New Testament constantly instructs the believer to act according to his or her belief: 'Let the same mind be in you as was in Jesus Christ.'"[18] We need to do better than this. We need a theology that does not invite us to forget that "the grace of God has appeared for the salvation of all men, training us to renounce irreligion and worldly passions, and to live sober, upright, and godly lives in this world, awaiting our blessed hope, the appearing of the glory of our great God and Savior Jesus Christ, who gave himself for us to redeem us from all iniquity and to purify for himself a people of his own who are zealous for good deeds" (Titus 2:11–14). We need a theology that does not invite us to act as if the incarnation, cross, and empty tomb have done nothing new and transforming in human history.

Fortunately, we do not have to create or invent this *ex nihilo;* to some degree, there is already such a Lutheran theology. Resources for this better theology exist, for example, in Article IV of the Apology of the Augsburg Confession. It has always been something of a mystery that Article IV, simply because it recurs regularly to the formula that the "law always accuses," should be read in a static, wooden fashion that ignores its own equally regular affirmations that the grace of God is a power that has accomplished something within the history of redemption in the lives of the baptized. The Apology teaches, of course, that the "fulfillment of the law, which follows our renewal, is scanty and impure," and that "the remnants of sin still cling" to us in this life (Ap IV, 159). But it never denies that something decisive has happened. Indeed, it affirms that renewal has begun and that, therefore, these remnants of sin "always accuse us unless by faith in Christ we take hold of the forgiveness of sins" (Ap IV, 159).

To be sure, Article IV does not answer all the questions that need to be answered. In considerable measure, it simply sets two understandings of the Christian life side by side, leaving us with the task of bringing them together in a coherent whole. There are, for example, places where Article IV clearly thinks of the Christian life as a constant return—again and again—to the promise of grace which faith grasps. "[W]hen we say that faith justifies, some will think that it refers to a foundational principle, namely, that faith is the beginning of justification or the preparation for justification. As a result, it is not by faith itself that we are accepted by God, but by the works that follow. . . . We do not think of faith in this way. Instead, we maintain that, properly and truly, by faith itself we are regarded as righteous for Christ's sake, that is, we are acceptable to God" (Ap IV, 71–72). Here, it is clear, the Apology depicts our righteousness as relational rather than substantive, as an either/or condition. Either one is wholly and entirely righteous because one has taken hold of the righteousness of Christ, or one attempts to stand before God simply on one's own—in which case, however good many of our actions may be when taken piecemeal, the person who does them is only a sinner, wholly under condemnation. And for the justified sinner who is right with God, good works are said to follow spontaneously, as the good tree produces good fruit. Moral reflection or instruction is really beside the point.

But there are also places—quite a few, in fact—where Article IV thinks of the Christian life as gradual growth in a righteousness that is acquired "more and more" as the Spirit of Christ empowers us. Thus, for example: "[W]e ought to begin to keep the law and then keep it more and more. Now, we are not talking about ceremonies, but about that law which deals with the impulses of the heart, namely, the Decalogue" (Ap IV, 124). Or again: "We openly confess, therefore, that the keeping of the law must begin in us and then increase more and more" (Ap IV, 136). Here, it is clear, one must go to work pruning and fertilizing the tree if one hopes for good fruit. Reflection, instruction, direction, and inculcation may all be needed. This kind of righteousness is not imputed but imparted. Not a matter of either/or, but a matter of bit-by-bit and more-and-more. It grows as the renewing power of Christ's Spirit begins to transform the impulses of our hearts. Something new has happened in the baptized. They are no longer in bondage to sin, and a new power is at work in their lives, setting them on the way toward the holiness Christ not only asks but also promises.

Having set these two understandings of the Christian's righteousness side by side, the Apology left to later generations the task of thinking through precisely how we are to use and do justice to both. Apart from dialectical Lutheranism, the standard Lutheran answer became that of Article III ("Concerning the Righteousness of Faith before God") of the Formula of Concord. Concerned to distinguish between justification and regeneration, it asserts that there must be a "proper order" between them—according to which order, renewal follows justification, not temporally but conceptually (FC, SD, III, 40–41).

This formulation, though not mistaken, turns out to be of relatively little help. Article III distinguishes the righteousness imputed in the gospel's promise of forgiveness from "being made righteous in fact and in truth on account of the love and other virtues infused into us through the Holy Spirit . . ." (FC, SD, III, 62).[19] The problem has always been that a strong commitment to the language of justification seems to undercut any need for the language of sanctification.[20] If grace has really pardoned sinners, clothing them in the righteousness of Christ than which there can be nothing more righteous, there seems little need any longer for grace to empower a journey toward holiness. We're already there! That holiness has already been given in Christ. What more could be needed? All that is left is for these good trees to bring forth good fruit, leaping in joyful spontaneity to the side of needy neighbors, and needing no instruction or guidance—or, alternatively, sinning contentedly in the sweet assurance that grace will abound. We always seem to arrive at this same dead end, with these same alternatives, neither of which has any place for obeying the commandments. And this produces a church entirely captive—both in what it affirms and in what it rejects—to the terms of the moral life prevailing in the surrounding culture.

Hence, the formula "justification followed by sanctification," accurate though it may be, never gets us very far. In making place for sanctification ("being made righteous in fact and in truth"), we seem to make justification a fiction. In emphasizing the reality of justification, we make it hard to explain what still needs doing in sanctification. We are always seeming to endanger the reality of one or the other.

IV

Lutheranism leaves us, therefore, with two contrasting depictions of the way grace works in our lives to make us righteous before God. According to one formulation, God's grace is a power working within us, bringing us ever more fully into that holiness of life without which no one will see the Lord. This holiness is not a *condition* for communion with God; rather, it is simply a *description* of what we must become before we can really want to be in God's presence. According to the second formulation, grace is not power but pardon. It is the word of forgiveness and acceptance to which we must return in faith again and again.

When Lutherans have asked themselves about the relation between these two kinds of righteousness—at least whenever they have not, in dialectical fashion, simply eliminated entirely the depiction of grace as a power making us holy—they have generally tried to say, as in Article III of the Formula of Concord, that sanctification follows justification, not temporally but conceptually, and that the proper order between the two must be maintained. But, as we have noted, this approach always seems to undermine the importance of either justification or sanctification. Can we do better?[21]

In an article titled "What Karl Barth Learned from Martin Luther," George Hunsinger, using language that I appropriated earlier, depicted two ways of thinking about the relation of grace and the Christian life—contrasting the "again and again" motif with the "more and more" motif. He did this in order to argue that Barth had, in fact, deliberately revived and reemphasized the "again and again" motif that had been pronounced in Luther's own understanding. "Nothing is more characteristic of Barth's soteriology than the thesis that grace is new to us as sinners each morning, . . . and that it does not arrive by portions and pieces, but comes to us again and again in the perfection of the finished work of Christ."[22] But Hunsinger also noticed an important respect in which Barth nevertheless differed somewhat from Luther, and it is our clue to the way forward. In contrast to Luther, Hunsinger wrote, Barth "elevated reconciliation to preeminence so that justification became a subordinate concept which described reconciliation as a whole—as also did sanctification, justification's simultaneous counterpart."[23] That is, these theological constructs give us two different languages with which to describe God's work of reconciliation.

The terms "justification" and "sanctification" point not to different works of God but to two different angles—pardon and power—from which to describe the one work of God in Christ, reconciling the world to himself. These are different ways of describing how God's Spirit draws our lives into the story of Jesus. The language of pardon addresses a truth of our experience—the continuing lure of sin. The language of power articulates the truth of reality—that God is at work, fulfilling his promise to turn sinners into saints. Our concern, therefore, should not be that justification must always precede sanctification, a word of pardon precede a word of power. The distinction between these works of the Holy Spirit lies not in their order but in the circumstances in which these different words of grace are needed and appropriate. To those who are troubled in their hearts and tempted to despair, God's word of grace must be spoken as sheer pardon, free of any demand that might be heard as accusation. Only grace as pardon can draw the despairing out of themselves, teach them not to look inward (which is, after all, their problem), but outward to the righteousness of Christ. To those who trust that by God's grace they are no longer in bondage to sin and who seek, however haltingly and imperfectly, to bring their lives into obedience to his will, the gift and guidance of God's empowering grace should be offered. Thus, the distinction between justification and sanctification lies not in some wooden order of priority but in the skill of discerning whether grace as pardon or as power is needed. And the distinction between these languages is not the chief structuring principle of theology; it is, rather, the pastor's art.[24]

How these two languages—these two understandings of our righteousness before God—can themselves be united or reconciled is God's own eschatological mystery.[25] We may be confident, however, that the one God—in whom it is always yes—who has graciously pardoned us, is himself committed to empowering us for holiness of life and will one day complete that task, as Luther himself makes clear in a wonderful extended metaphor:

> It is similar to the case of a sick man who believes the doctor who promises him a sure recovery and in the meantime obeys the doctor's order in the hope of the promised recovery and abstains from those things which have been forbidden him, so that he may in no way hinder the promised return to health or increase his sickness until the doctor can fulfill his promise to him. Now is this sick man well? The fact is that he is both sick and well at the same time. He is sick in fact, but he is well because of the sure promise of the doctor, whom he trusts and who has reckoned him as already cured, because he is sure that he will cure him; for he has already begun to cure him and no longer reckons to him a sickness unto death. In the same way

Christ, our Samaritan, has brought His half-dead man into the inn to be cared for, and He has begun to heal him, . . . but in the meantime in the hope of the promised recovery He prohibits him from doing or omitting things by which his cure might be impeded. . . . Now, is he perfectly righteous? No, for he is at the same time both a sinner and a righteous man; a sinner in fact, but a righteous man by the sure imputation and promise of God that He will continue to deliver him from sin until He has completely cured him. And thus he is entirely healthy in hope, but in fact he is still a sinner; but he has the beginning of righteousness, so that he continues more and more always to seek it. . . .[26]

Christians may often experience their life as a daily return— again and again, new every morning—to the word of pardon that gives them hope. But the report of that *experience*, crucial as it is, must not subvert the truth of *reality*—that within the inn of his church, God is at work forming people whose hearts are set to obey. These are not people who suppose that they can ever face the judgment of God secure in their own deeds and character; rather, these are people in whom there has begun to be, as Paul Ramsey put it, "a combination of increasing humility and increasing achievement."[27] The more God's grace empowers their lives, the more they know their need of his pardon. And the word of pardon carries with it God's commitment to make us people who will want to live in his presence—to make us what he says we are. Hence, God's promise is embedded in his command: "You shall be holy."

Until that day, of course, we continue to exist within the "simul"—as simultaneously saint and sinner. We dare not, however, contentedly accept this as our normal and appropriate condition—as if God did not intend one day to have done with the "simul," and were not already at work on that project here and now. As Barth says, the people of God, as the "living community of the Lord Jesus," must be "horrified by the dishonor that is done to God in that *simul* relation."[28] We should therefore pray that the power of God's perfecting grace may day by day, more and more, have its effect in our lives. Not to pray that seriously is not to take seriously God's own commitment to make us holy. "The wakeful church and its wakeful members pray 'Hallowed be thy name,'" Barth writes, "even though all around them, uttered even by themselves sometimes in their waking dreams, there continues the apathetic and monotonous murmur: 'At one and the same time both righteous and sinner, world without end. Amen.' No, the living community and its members cannot say Amen to this."[29]

We should pray God to put an end to the "*simul*," that our hearts may be set to obey. The command of God, which calls for our obedience, comes to us day by day as the command of the One whose grace has been revealed in the face of Jesus Christ. And because that is true, because we can and must say "Amen" to him, we should listen for the promise in the commands of the Decalogue: You *shall* love the Lord your God with all your heart, soul, and mind. You *shall* become a child who loves the Father, a bride eager to greet her bridegroom, a creature who loves the Creator from whom comes life and every good thing, a lover of God in whose speech the praise of God resounds. All this . . . you *shall* be. And to trust that promise—the promise that we shall become people whose hearts are set to obey God's commandments—is both our duty and our delight.

Notes

1. An earlier version of this chapter appeared under the same title, "Hearts Set to Obey," as pp. 253–75 in Carl E. Braaten and Christopher R. Seitz (eds.), *I Am the Lord Your God: Christian Reflections on the Ten Commandments* (Grand Rapids: Eerdmans, 2005).

2. Indeed, a similar issue can occur in other than Christian contexts. See, for example, the mention (in section III, chapter 1 above) of the Moroccan Jews who underwent forced conversion to Islam in the twelfth century.

3. Formula of Concord, Solid Declaration, VI, 15, in *The Book of Concord*, ed. Robert Kolb and Timothy J. Wengert (Minneapolis: Fortress Press, 2000).

4. The brief summary in this and the two preceding paragraphs of what we might call Old Testament ethics relies on Walter Brueggemann, *Reverberations of Faith: A Theological Handbook of Old Testament Themes* (Louisville: Westminster John Knox Press, 2002), pp. 66–69.

5. Dietrich Bonhoeffer, *Psalms: The Prayer Book of the Bible* (Minneapolis: Augsburg Publishing House, 1970), p. 31.

6. This is the issue explored in helpful detail by Robert P. Scharlemann, *Thomas Aquinas and John Gerhard* (New Haven and London: Yale University Press, 1964). Scharlemann characterizes Gerhard's theology as one that focused on situations of extreme anxiety. He notes, however, that Gerhard himself saw a possible "way out" of this narrow focus, but it was a way that he did not

finally take. He might, Scharlemann writes, have regarded "the extreme situations of which he speaks as universally possible but not necessarily universally actual" (p. 240).

7. Einar Billing, *Our Calling* (Philadelphia: Fortress Press, 1964), p. 35.

8. John Witte, Jr., *Law and Protestantism: The Legal Teachings of the Lutheran Reformation* (Cambridge: Cambridge University Press, 2002), p. 92.

9. Ibid., p. 170.

10. David S. Yeago, "Gnosticism, Antinomianism, and Reformation Theology," *Pro Ecclesia*, 2 (Winter 1993), p. 38.

11. Cambridge University Press, 2001. Citations of *Christian Contradictions* will be given by page number in parentheses within the body of the text.

12. Anthony Lane says of Hampson's work: "Her approach would be followed by many, but by no means all, Lutherans" (*Justification by Faith in Catholic-Protestant Dialogue* [London & New York: T & T Clark, 2002], p. 3, n. 1). In the same context, however, Lane writes: "Reading the *Formula of Concord* on this topic [i.e., justification] I am struck by how much common ground there is with Calvin's exposition and how relatively marginal are the differences" (p. 4). This suggests what is, I think, the case—that those Lutherans who take an approach something like Hampson's are drawing on certain aspects of Luther's theology, but that a wider sample of both Luther and Lutheranism would demonstrate how unstable is any theology built on those aspects alone.

13. Lest we think these issues too simple, we should note that Roman Catholic moral theology may face the opposite problem. Having for so long focused its attention on ways in which character is formed by (right or wrong) acts, the tradition of Catholic moral theology has struggled to articulate a sense in which the person as a whole stands before God as saint or sinner and is not just a collection of acts. See John Mahoney, *The Making of Moral Theology* (Oxford: Clarendon Press, 1987). For an argument to the effect that this problem was not entirely overcome in the moral teaching of Pope John Paul II, see chapter 1 in this volume. For a perceptive articulation of how "revisionist" trends in Roman Catholic moral theology may go too far and—like dialectical Lutheranism—lose the importance of particular acts in the moral life, see Darlene Fozard Weaver, "Taking Sin Seriously," *Journal of Religious Ethics*, 31 (Spring 2003), pp. 45–74.

14. The contrast between a righteousness that is, under grace, gradually acquired "more and more," and a righteousness that is simply given "again and again" as one returns to the starting point, to the pardoning word of grace, is not specifically Hampson's language. It is, however, helpful for clarifying the two frameworks of thought. I have appropriated this language from George Hunsinger's essay "What Karl Barth Learned from Martin Luther," pp. 279–304 in *Disruptive Grace: Studies in the Theology of Karl Barth* (Grand Rapids: Eerdmans, 2000). Cf., especially, pp. 299–300. In some of the other writings cited in footnote 1, I have—to make much the same sort of point—contrasted the Christian life as "journey" with the Christian life as "dialogue."

15. Scharlemann, pp. 226–27.

16. Of course, characterizing Lutheran theology as fundamentally "paradoxical" is, to some degree, a rather recent phenomenon—fruit of the enormous influence of H. Richard Niebuhr's typology in *Christ and Culture* (Harper & Row, 1951). Interestingly, however, Scharlemann notes a sense in which Gerhard's narrowed focus actually removes from Aquinas's view what is "genuinely paradoxical" (p. 154). Gerhard will not puzzle with Aquinas over the paradox of how divine and human agency somehow interpenetrate and cooperate in human action; agency must belong to one or the other, and the movement of the will in conversion is "either of God or of man" (p. 159). This suggests to Scharlemann that "the concept of free will has, in Gerhard's thinking, lost virtually all of the dialectical and paradoxical functions which it had in the Thomistic use" (p. 159). Although Scharlemann also notes (p. 182) a way in which paradox reappears in Gerhard's thought, this is, indeed, an interesting subversion of our normal characterizations.

17. Cf. Oliver O'Donovan, *The Problem of Self-Love in St. Augustine* (New Haven and London: Yale University Press, 1980), p. 158. Cf. also Hampson, p. 35: "Salvation and the doctrine of creation are one and the same thing, to be placed on one side of what I have called the 'dialectic.'"

18. Niels Henrik Gregersen, "Ten Theses on the Future of Lutheran Theology: Charisms, Contexts, and Challenges," *Dialog*, 41 (Winter 2002), p. 268.

19. Thus, commenting on Romans 4:7, Luther says of those whose sin is forgiven: "They are actually sinners, but they are righteous by the imputation of a merciful God. . . . [T]hey are sinners in fact but righteous in hope" (*Luther's Works*, vol. 25, p. 258).

20. Cf. Hampson, p. 62: "By their very nature imputation and transformational change would seem to obviate the need for the other."

21. I am not so foolish as to suppose that what follows is a new creation. When we work on a problem that has engaged so many serious Christian thinkers over the centuries, our first concern should hardly be creativity. The approach I take in the following paragraphs bears at least some resemblance to what has sometimes been called the "double justification" formula on which (some) Catholics and Protestants (including Melanchthon) reached agreement at the Regensburg Colloquy in 1541. That colloquy was the last serious attempt to avoid a permanently divided church before the Council of Trent made such a hope futile. See Steven Ozment, *The Age of Reform 1250–1550* (New Haven and London: Yale University Press, 1980), pp. 377–78, 405–6. (We should note that Anthony Lane [p. 58] denies that the Regensburg formula is properly characterized as "double justification." Rather, its references to imputed and inherent righteousness are, according to Lane, "simply ways of describing justification and sanctification.") My own approach differs, I think, from the "double justification" formula (if we wish to call it that) in that (1) I leave any final reconciliation of these two "languages" to God and accept the need to distinguish their use in pastoral practice; (2) I emphasize (following Barth) that this final reconciliation must somehow involve the fact that these are simply two different angles on the one reconciling work of God, even if the angles must remain somewhat distinct in Christian experience in this life; and (3) I am clear that the Catholic emphasis on internal transformation points to the *reality* that God is accomplishing, even while the Lutheran emphasis on an extrinsic righteousness which must be grasped by faith is (at some moments) essential for Christians who are only on the way toward the reality God has promised to accomplish.

22. Hunsinger, p. 300.

23. Ibid., p. 304.

24. Anthony Lane has made a similar point in describing the differing "concerns" with which Protestants and Catholics come to a discussion of sanctification. "Protestants are concerned to emphasize our continuing need of mercy and the assurance that comes from the imputed righteousness of Christ and fear anything that detracts from the finished work of Christ on the cross. Catholics are concerned to emphasize the reality of the transformation that Christ brings and fear the idea of a purely external righteousness and anything that detracts from the effective work of the Holy Spirit in our lives" (*Justification by Faith in Catholic-Protestant Dialogue*, p. 12).

25. This, in fact, is the most important way in which the "simul" must retain a place in Christian theology. Until the end of the age, Christians will need to talk of God's gracious work in two—different, but equally essential—ways: as both pardon and power.

26. *Luther's Works*, volume 25: *Lectures on Romans*, p. 260.

27. Paul Ramsey, *Basic Christian Ethics* (New Y:ork Charles Scribner's Sons, 1950), p. 200. Ramsey adds: "This has been the hall-mark of Christian character in all ages."

28. Karl Barth, *The Christian Life* (Grand Rapids: Eerdmans, 1981), pp. 153–54.

29. Ibid., p. 154.

3

Amazing Grace[1]

"Theology is ecclesial, or it is nothing at all. And if each Church remains faithful to Revelation, 'thinking its doctrines through to the end,' both sides might come to agreement at some specific spot. Says Barth: 'Let the Roman Catholic Church think through its doctrine on nature and grace, and the teaching on justification that was developed by Trent.' And to him we say: 'Let reformation theology think through its teaching on the visible Church, on obedience and law, and also its dialectic about *homo simul peccator et justus*. Then life will begin to flow through the Church's limbs. Questions will be posed, and the possibility of an answer will be real once again.'"[2]

That in Jesus Christ God has freely and graciously become friend of sinners and justifier of the ungodly is the heart of the Christian gospel and the center of Christian life. It would be hard to imagine Christian hymnody without its praise for this divine grace to sinners. "How vast your mercy to accept / The burden of our sin, / And bow your head in cruel death / To make us clean within," says a hymn dating (in its Latin version) from the eighth century. The wonder of grace is, as we might expect, a staple of hymns inspired by Reformation teaching. "Salvation unto us has come / By God's free grace and favor." In the bleeding Savior on the tree Isaac Watts discerned "[a]mazing pity, grace unknown, / And love beyond degree." "There's a Wideness in God's Mercy," written by Frederick Faber, a nineteenth-century convert from Anglicanism to Roman Catholicism, affirms, even, that "[t]here is grace enough for thousands / of new worlds as great as this," and the reformed slave trader, John Newton, believed he had experienced an "Amazing Grace" capable of saving even "a wretch like me."

The language of worship must, of course, sometimes be given greater precision in the language of dogmatic theology, and this is surely true for ethics as a branch of dogmatics. Questions about how God's grace works in human beings to produce a transformation that involves, as St. Paul writes in Romans 12, the renewal of their minds and a discernment of God's will are among the most complicated and controverted of issues in Christian theology.

From among the many topics one might take up in an essay on the place of grace in the Christian life, I will focus here on three: (1) the necessity of God's prevenient grace if the power of sin is to be overcome and we are really to *love* God, (2) the relation of grace and *faith* in bringing about the justification and renewal of sinners, and (3) the contours of a life that is energized by confidence in divine grace already bestowed in Jesus, but, at the same time, lived in *hope*. Although this will leave much unsaid, it nevertheless draws into the orbit of grace many important themes of Christian moral reflection. It gives us one angle on the three chief theological virtues, it takes up themes deeply embedded in the scriptures, and it directs our attention to topics that have been stumbling blocks for ecumenical understanding and agreement.

I: "Apart from me you can do nothing"

Jesus's words in John 15:5, which became so important to Augustine as he wrestled with Pelagianism, direct us to grace as the starting point of the Christian life. Taken in the abstract, of course, the claim that apart from God human beings can do nothing raises far-reaching questions about the genuineness of human freedom. And, in fact, it has always been difficult for Christian thinkers to be simultaneously anti-Manichaean and anti-Pelagian. In the face of a quite natural, recurring (Manichaean) tendency to make sense of human moral experience by describing our human nature as a battleground between good and evil principles, Christian thinkers will want to assert human power of choice. In the face of an equally natural (Pelagian) desire to take seriously this created power of choice as the moving force in the moral life, Christian thinkers will want to assert that, apart from God's grace, our power of choice is always governed by the direction of our will, which is now enslaved to sin. So many loves—some clearly good, others suspect—come quite naturally to us, and we may be uncertain how to love with a whole heart or whether we are capable of such love.

The division within sinful human beings is memorably depicted by St. Paul in Romans 7(18–19). "I can will what is right, but I cannot do it. For I do not do the good I want, but the evil I do not want is what I do." Although interpreters will probably always disagree about who the "I" of Romans 7 is, I think it best to read Paul as depicting here the divided will (not of those who are in Christ, but) of children of Adam; for Romans 6 makes clear that Christians are no longer to be described as enslaved to sin, and Romans 8:2 asserts that the indwelling Spirit of Jesus "has set me free from the law of sin and death."

Perhaps the most memorable description of the divided will comes in Augustine's *Confessions,* when he depicts his struggle to give himself wholeheartedly to God and his inability to accomplish this simply by willing to do it. Having heard the story of Victorinus—himself a scholar and rhetorician like Augustine, who, upon becoming a Christian, had made public profession of his faith—Augustine writes,

> I was on fire to be like him, . . . but I was held back, and I was
> held back not by fetters put on me by someone else, but by
> the iron bondage of my own will. . . . And the new will which I

was beginning to have and which urged me to worship you in freedom and to enjoy you, God, the only certain joy, was not yet strong enough to overpower the old will. . . . So my two wills, one old, one new, one carnal, one spiritual, were in conflict, and they wasted my soul by their discord.[3]

He could not order his loves rightly simply by willing to do so, because, as he notes, "I, no doubt, was on both sides" (8.5). The division cut so deeply into his soul that he could not, by his own power, simply place himself on one side or the other. Only later, after the climactic scene in the garden, would it be the case that when "I willed, I should will it thoroughly" (8.8).

The grace of God alone can overcome this division within the self, and—though it is true that such a strong theology of grace gives rise to a number of difficulties, a few of which I consider below—we should not be so concerned about the difficulties that we miss the importance of divine grace for Christian ethics. Robert Merrihew Adams has called attention to a "gaping hole" in most modern ethical theories. "They have nothing to say to us in a situation of helplessness."[4] Adams is concerned chiefly to commend the moral significance of actions which, though seemingly pointless, carry symbolic value, but his observation can be extended to the whole of the moral life. Learning to love the good, to bring into right order our fragmented and dispersed loves, and to overcome our idolatrous loves, is a task that may well evoke in us a sense of helplessness. We may be forced to say, with Augustine, "I, no doubt, . . . [am] on both sides." An ethical theory that cannot speak to such helplessness "abandons us in what is literally the hour of our greatest need."[5]

It is also true, however, that a theology of grace raises problems for Christian ethics. Most obviously, perhaps, it may lead us to wonder whether human beings ever act freely and whether, in avoiding Pelagianism, we may flirt with a Manichaean depiction of our nature as entirely lacking the power of choice. Although Luther's *Bondage of the Will* admits of varying interpretations and may not be internally consistent, there are moments in the argument when such flirtation seems present. For example, his well-known image of the human will as a "beast of burden" might be thought to leave no room for the power of choice. "If God rides it, it wills and goes where God wills. . . . If Satan rides it, it wills and goes where Satan wills; nor can it choose to run to either of the two riders or to seek him out, but the riders themselves contend for the possession and control of it."[6]

It should perhaps not surprise us that at other moments Luther draws back and looks for ways to do justice to a distinctively human power of choice through which God's grace can work. "For heaven, as the saying goes, was not made for geese."[7] We should, I think, join Luther in those moments when he draws back and say something not unlike what Augustine says in Book 5 of *City of God*, where two issues concern him. One is whether we can sensibly speak of human freedom if God knows the future. Augustine's answer—a good one—is that among the causes God foreknows are our choices. "It does not follow, then, that there is nothing in our will because God foreknew what was going to be in our will; for if he foreknew this, it was not nothing that he foreknew."[8]

The more difficult question, however, is whether God causes to be what comes to be through our choices (which God foreknows). We may freely choose, Augustine says, but only God gives the power of achievement (5.10). Here, I suspect, we confront mysteries that are more than problems to be solved. It may help if we think of human life as a drama, whose author is God, and in which we play the parts given us. Having created characters of the sort we are, the author cannot simply manipulate them—at least not if he wishes to write well. But perhaps a sufficiently inventive author may still be able to incorporate all his characters' choices into the plot of a story that ends in accord with his design.

Dorothy Sayers, herself the author of both stories and plays, explores such an analogy with great ingenuity in *The Mind of the Maker*. An author has both characters and plot with which to work, but bringing them together in a coherent and satisfying story is no easy task. Sayers grants that authors have far more control over their characters than parents have over their children. But even of characters in a story it is true, she writes, that "unless the author permits them to develop in conformity with their proper nature, they will cease to be true and living crea-tures."[9] Indeed, "the free will of a genuinely created character has a certain reality, which the writer will defy at his peril."[10] Suppose the plot of the story seems to require from characters behavior that is simply not "in character." What then? An author may "behave like an autocratic deity and compel the characters to do his will whether or not," but this, of course, is unlikely to make for a good story. Alternatively, "[t]he humanistic and sensitive author may prefer to take the course of sticking to his characters and altering the plot to suit their development. This will result in a less violent shock to the reader's sense of reality, but also in an alarming incoherence of structure."[11] The right way out of such difficulties—requiring authorial skill of the highest order—permits characters to act in accord with their natures, while yet bringing the plot to the ending the author had envisioned. "In language to which we are accustomed in other connections," Sayers concludes, "neither predestination nor free will is everything, but, if the will acts freely in accordance with its true nature, it achieves by grace and not by judgment the eternal will of its maker, though possibly by a process un-like, and longer than, that which might have been imposed upon it by force."[12]

The genuineness of human volition is not the only issue, how-ever. A strong theology of grace, because it seems to obliterate all penultimate distinctions in the light of the ultimate either/or of God's verdict, may also seem sometimes to paralyze our powers of moral judgment and render us unable or unwilling to acknowledge moral goodness when we see it. It may, in Rein-hold Niebuhr's terms, make us "indifferent to relative moral discriminations."[13] Even the best of human achievements is tainted by our sin and falls short of the perfect love God wants from us; therefore, a strong theology of grace is "always in danger of heightening religious tension to the point where it breaks the moral tension, from which all decent action flows."[14]

This issue, though in different terms, came to the center of theological attention in the Protestant Reformation with the question of whether sin remains in the Christian. Roman Catholics answered that sin, in its most precise sense, does not remain. Although an inclination to sin (concupiscence) does remain even in Christians, the Holy Spirit dwells within them and, hence, there can be nothing in them that God condemns. The Council of Trent's Decree concerning original sin states the position clearly.

> If anyone denies that by the grace of our Lord Jesus Christ which is conferred in baptism, the guilt of original sin is remitted, or says that the whole of that which belongs to the essence of sin is not taken away, but says that it is only canceled or not imputed, let him be anathema. For in those who are born again God hates nothing. . . . But this holy council perceives and confesses that in the one baptized there remains concupiscence or an inclination to sin, which, since it is left for us to wrestle with, cannot injure those who do not acquiesce but resist manfully by the grace of Jesus Christ. . . .[15]

In the "Joint Declaration on the Doctrine of Justification," confirmed in 1999, Lutherans and Roman Catholics sought a way past this anathema. Thus, when Lutherans say that those who are justified are still sinners and that their sin constitutes opposition to God, "they do not deny that, despite this sin, they are not separated from God and that this sin is a "ruled" sin [that is, the believer is no longer enslaved by it]."[16] Roman Catholics, on the other hand, do not deny that remaining concupiscence (which they decline to call sin) "is objectively in contradiction to God and remains one's enemy in lifelong struggle" (4.4, 30). The issue is "whether man's historical existence is such that he can ever, by any discipline of reason or by any merit of grace, confront a divine judgment upon his life with an easy conscience."[17]

Perhaps we cannot do so—and should not. Without the Lutheran emphasis, therefore, Christian ethics is always in danger of appearing too self-contained, too ready to assume divine grace—and then move on. But, as Anthony Lane notes, we also need the finely grained moral distinctions between better and worse if there is to be any Christian ethical reflection at all:

> On the one hand it is true that we are all sinners, all in need of God's mercy. But if that is all we can say we end up with a

moral relativism. . . . It would have been wrong, for example, for white South Africans under apartheid to deflect criticism with the, doubtless true, statement that deep down all people are racists.[18]

Christian ethics can scarcely deny that divine grace—the indwelling power of the Holy Spirit—makes a difference, a moral difference, in our lives and loves.

Even apart from the gracious bestowal of the Holy Spirit which leads ultimately to salvation, we may well—with the Calvinist strand of Christian thought—speak also of "common" grace: a "non-salvific attitude of divine favor toward all human beings."[19] This common grace has generally been thought to include the many natural blessings which God bestows on his creatures as well as the ability even of unbelievers to do acts that serve the common good. One might, of course, speak of these as the work of providence rather than grace; yet, it does not seem wrong to think of them as unmerited blessings of the Creator. Calvin, in fact, speaking in particular of the gift of reason and understanding, writes that we ought to see in it "the peculiar grace of God."[20]

More significant for Christian ethics, however, would be a category of common grace that includes the moral worth of our actions. Probing just this possibility, Richard Mouw invites us to consider a case such as the following: Suppose a marriage between non-Christians has been broken by wrongdoing but is now repaired and reconciled through patient love and forgiveness. Christian theology would not say that this husband and wife are saved (or justified) when they rebuild their marriage; nevertheless, Christians who see the hand of God at work in human life may be inclined to discern here the presence of a healing grace. We want to say, Mouw suggests, that "God judges the inner states of the unbelieving couple who have experienced marital reconciliation to be better than the inner states associated with their former alienation. . . ."[21] Hence, from one angle—an important angle—we want and need to say that these spouses, whether reconciled or unreconciled in their marriage, are not in right relation with God apart from the gracious gift of the

Holy Spirit. But we need another angle of vision as well—enabling us to acknowledge that even God is not indifferent to the relative moral discriminations we must make in judging human action.

II: "God's love has been poured into our hearts through the Holy Spirit which has been given to us."

These words of St. Paul in Romans 5:5 point toward what has been perhaps the deepest (and most ecumenically divisive) problem in Christian reflection on the meaning of divine grace and the role of faith. In his influential tracing of the interactions of agape and eros in Christian thought, Anders Nygren rightly notes that Augustine "delights" to quote Romans 5:5 in order to describe how, through the work of the Holy Spirit, God infuses the grace of renewal, thereby giving to believers what he has commanded and making possible ascent to fellowship with God on the basis of holiness.[22] For Nygren this understanding of grace is a distortion of the true agape motif, but, interestingly, he can use the same passage from Romans to describe—favorably in his view—how St. Paul regards agape as a kind of divine "pneumatic fluid" which is infused into believers and, through them, passed on to others.[23] Even their own agapeic works, it seems, are really God's work—which is one way to be certain that human "works" do not displace grace in theological ethics.

We need only contrast Nygren's way of organizing our understanding of the Christian life with Kenneth Kirk's equally wide-ranging and learned depiction of life as a journey toward the vision of God to begin to appreciate just how deep this issue goes.[24] Is grace fundamentally a *gift* bestowed by God, and the Christian's grace-given faith, then, formed by love? Or is grace fundamentally God's *favor* toward sinners, and the Christian's response one of faith that trusts this promised favor? The first approach risks constantly turning our attention inward—to how we are doing or what moral progress we are making—and such an inward turn is, of course, precisely a turn away from the power of grace that comes from outside us. The second approach risks depicting the Christian life as resting content in our sinful condition as if it were acceptable to a gracious God.

We may, of course, want to say "yes" to both of these ways of structuring the Christian life, while doing our best to avoid their dangers, and that may be wise. History shows, though, that this is by no means easy. That the Bible often speaks of God's grace as favor toward sinners, and that therefore the Reformation emphasis must be affirmed, is beyond dispute. It is also true, however, that the Bible—and even St. Paul—can think of grace as a gift bestowed on and infused into believers. Thus, in his greeting at the outset of 1 Corinthians, St. Paul writes: "I give thanks to God always for you because of the grace [charis] of God which was given you in Christ Jesus, . . . so that you are not lacking in any spiritual gift [charism]." The favor of God, enacted and displayed in Jesus, takes form and shape in the character of believers.

In this, as so often, St. Augustine has already displayed the rough contours of our problem. Thus, for example, in his important treatise "On the Spirit and the Letter," he notes that the righteousness of God of which St. Paul speaks is not that by which God himself is righteous—a standard that we must attain—but "that with which He endows man when He justifies the ungodly."[25] Hence, God's righteousness is not a requirement but a free gift. Nevertheless, in Augustine's formulation cited above, this gift is not simply the *favor Dei* which we are invited to rely upon and trust. It is something more like a substantive endowment, a healing of the interior person.[26] The gift of grace is placed in service of healing and renewal. "The law was therefore given, in order that grace might be sought; grace was given, in order that the law might be fulfilled."[27]

The Scholastic distinction between uncreated and created grace deals in different language with similar concerns. "Uncreated grace" refers to the favor of God, which, through the indwelling of the Holy Spirit, effects a created habit of grace within the soul. It is this habit of soul that fits one for God's presence and is the basis of justification. But one need only read Karl Rahner's intricate essay "Some Implications of the

Scholastic Concept of Uncreated Grace" to begin to appreciate how difficult it is to describe in a satisfactory way the relation between uncreated and created grace. Shall we say—as, Rahner notes, St. Paul seems to suggest—that what comes first is the indwelling of the Holy Spirit (uncreated grace), and that the Spirit, in turn, creates in believers an inner quality of righteousness or a habit of grace? Shall we say, in other words, that every created grace is a "consequence and a manifestation of the possession of this uncreated grace"?[28] Or shall we say, as Rahner characterizes Scholastic teaching, that the Holy Spirit can dwell in believers only insofar as their very person has been renewed—in short, that apart from created grace no indwelling of the Spirit could be possible?

In the *Summa Theologiae* Aquinas resolves the issue in the following manner: Even though grace is indeed God's gracious favor, which can hardly be possessed or disposed of by human beings, it is also what Thomas O'Meara has called "a form of life," and not just a transitory divine favor provided again and again.[29] In q. 110, a. 1 of the *Prima Secundae* of the *Summa* Aquinas asks whether grace "set[s] up something" in the human soul—in particular, whether divine grace can become a "quality" of the human soul. Distinguishing various uses of the term "grace," Aquinas notes first how it may refer to the love or favorable attitude that one person has toward another, "as we might say that this soldier has the king's grace and favor." It may also, however, mean a gift that is given freely, "as we might say, 'I confer on you this grace.'" And the crucial question, then, is whether the first of these meanings implies or requires the second, whether grace does indeed "set up" something in the soul. Aquinas holds that it does, even though the first objection he considers in q. 110, a. 1 states (as clearly as Luther could have) why one might think otherwise:

> It seems that grace does not set up something in the soul. For as a man is said to have the grace and favour of God, so too he is said to have the grace and favour of man. . . . Now when a man is said to have the grace and favour of a man, nothing is set up in the one who has the other's grace; but in the one whose

grace he has there is set up a certain approval. Therefore when a man is said to have God's grace, nothing is set up in his soul; all that is signified is a divine approval.

To this objection Aquinas replies by distinguishing between the way in which one has the favor of another human being and the way in which one has God's favor.

> Even when someone is said to have man's grace and favour, it is implied that there is something in him pleasing to man, just as when someone is said to have God's grace and favour; but there is a difference. For what is pleasing to us in someone else is presupposed to our love for him; but what is pleasing to God is caused by the divine love. . . .

That is, even the "form of life," the "quality" that is "set up" in the soul and becomes one's possession, permitting us to say that one "has God's grace" (*gratiam Dei habere*), even this quality is a supernatural gift that has first been given by God (*a Deo proveniens*). It is this quality of the soul that, fully developed, fits one for God's presence. It is not simply God's favorable attitude toward us; it is a "form of life," a gift that takes up residence within the person's character. But to speak of this gift simply as our possession would hardly be adequate. Better to say, as Theo Kobusch does in explicating Aquinas: "The absolutely nonmanipulable is present only in the mode of gift (*donum*)."[30]

Likewise, Luther's view, though surely emphasizing grace as divine favor toward sinners, is much more complex than has sometimes been appreciated. Thus, for example, in "Against Latomus," an important early treatise, he distinguishes (and relates) what he calls "grace" and "gift."

> A righteous and faithful man doubtless has both grace and the gift. Grace makes him wholly pleasing so that his person is wholly accepted, . . . but the gift heals from sin and from all his corruption of body and soul. . . . Everything is forgiven through grace, but as yet not everything is healed through the gift. The gift has been infused, the leaven has been added to the mixture. It works so as to purge away the sin for which a person has

already been forgiven. . . . A person neither pleases, nor has grace, except on account of the gift which labors in this way to cleanse from sin.[31]

If the language is not that of the Scholastics, perhaps the patterns of thought are not as far removed from each other as we have sometimes supposed.

Hence, we would paint far too neat a picture if we were simply to play off against each other grace as divine favor (external to us) and grace as (interior) divine gift—and think of these as Reformation versus Roman Catholic emphases. For, while the languages are very different—returning "again and again" to the promised grace, or growing "more and more" in the grace that has been given—the structural problems are related.[32] It is not easy to understand, in Luther's language, why one who is the object of God's favor, who is pleasing to God, need purge away sin or do anything more than, simply, trust that good news. It is not easy to understand, in Aquinas's language, why one in whom a new, supernatural form of life has taken root need return time and again with renewed faith to the promise that, despite his sinful inclinations, God looks on him with favor. If we emphasize our need to return again and again to the promise of God's favor, we seem to undermine the love of God that has been poured into our hearts through the Holy Spirit. If we emphasize the sense in which this new life of love becomes more and more our possession, becomes habitual, we seem to undermine the sense in which it is, finally, God's continuing gift and work in us. Neither emphasis is entirely safe without the other.

Reinhold Niebuhr helpfully distinguishes "two aspects of the life of grace," which he calls "grace as power" and "grace as pardon."[33] Noting that it is always difficult to express both aspects of the experience of grace without seeming to do an injustice to one or the other, Niebuhr writes: "The theologies which have sought to do justice to the fact that saints nevertheless remain sinners have frequently, perhaps usually, obscured the indeterminate possibilities of realizations of good in both individual and collective life. The theologies which have sought to do justice to the positive aspects of regeneration have usually obscured the realities of sin which appear on every new level of virtue."[34] One way to understand much of Karl Barth's doctrine of reconciliation in volume IV of his *Church Dogmatics* is to read him as trying to give full expression to both aspects of grace. He "elevated reconciliation to preeminence so that justification became a subordinate concept which described reconciliation as a whole—as also did sanctification, justification's simultaneous counterpart."[35]

This is, I suspect, the best Christian ethics can manage or should try to manage. The one gracious work of God in Christ, reconciling the world to himself, will—this side of the eschaton—always have to be described in the languages of both pardon and power. These are different but necessary ways of describing how God's Spirit draws human lives into the story of Jesus. The language of pardon speaks to Christians' continuing experience of sin in their lives; the language of power reflects the truth that the Spirit of Christ does, indeed, dwell in believers. Both languages will, therefore, be necessary to say everything that needs to be said about the place of grace in Christian life.

In adopting this position I am returning to something like the "double justification" formula on which (some) Catholics and (some) Protestants reached agreement at the Regensburg Colloquy in 1541.[36] That colloquy, the last serious attempt to avoid a permanently divided church before the decisions of the Council of Trent made such a hope futile, affirmed that "living faith is that which both appropriates mercy in Christ, believing that the righteousness which is in Christ is freely imputed to it, and at the same time receives the promise of the Holy Spirit and love."[37] More than 450 years later, in the "Joint Declaration on the Doctrine of Justification," Lutherans and Catholics adopted a formula not unlike that of Regensburg: "We confess together that God forgives sin by grace and at the same time frees human beings from sin's enslaving power and imparts the gift of new life in Christ. When persons come by faith to share in Christ, God no longer imputes to them their sin and through the Holy Spirit effects in them an active love. These two aspects of God's gracious action are not to be separated . . ."

4.2, 22). We are not likely to do much better than this in our own attempts to distinguish without separating the *charis* and the *charism* bestowed on those who are in Christ.

III: "Through him we have obtained access to this grace in which we stand, and we rejoice in our hope of sharing the glory of God."

These words of St. Paul in Romans 5:2 invite us to consider the relation between the grace bestowed on believers and the future glory for which they hope. Although salvation is a gift that has, in some sense, already been bestowed on believers, it is also a future state not yet attained, toward which one must "press on," as Philippians 3:12 puts it. The object is not, of course, simply one's personal salvation. It is the reign of God inaugurated in Jesus's death and resurrection but still to be revealed for every eye to see. Yet, however certain is the fact that God's rule will one day be manifested, confidence that any of us in particular will be saved and share in that reign might seem to be premature or presumptuous. For within human history Christians are always "on the way," and we need to discern how this truth determines the contours of a life pleasing to God.

Grace having been bestowed in Jesus Christ, we ought to live with confidence that God will make good on the promise of which the Spirit of Jesus serves as down payment. The reign of God not yet having been manifested, however, we must "press on" toward something that is present now chiefly as the object of our hope. To "press on" or to "hope" must mean more than just to "await" or "anticipate." It suggests difficulty while on the way, and it might seem even to suggest uncertainty of outcome. Were there no uncertainty, after all, why would one need the virtue of hope? Then expectation would suffice. Yet it is "hope of sharing the glory of God" that St. Paul commends even to those who have already through Jesus "obtained access to this grace in which we stand."

Precisely what to say about the character of Christian hope has not been easy to work out. Thus, for example, a decree from the sixth session of the Council of Trent, while readily granting that "no pious person ought to doubt the mercy of God, the merit of Christ and the virtue and efficacy of the sacraments," nonetheless asserts of believers that "each one, when he considers himself and his own weakness and indisposition, may have fear and apprehension concerning his own grace, since no one can know with the certainty of faith, which cannot be subject to error, that he has obtained the grace of God."[38] The cadence seems quite different in John Wesley's famous description of his Aldersgate experience: "I felt my heart strangely warmed. I felt I did trust in Christ, Christ alone for my salvation; and an assurance was given me that he had taken away *my* sins, even *mine*, and saved *me* from the law of sin and death."[39] That same assurance is nicely articulated in a stanza from one of Charles Wesley's hymns:

> By faith we know thee strong to save
> (Save us, a present Savior thou!)
> Whate'er we hope, by faith we have,
> Future and past subsisting now.

Take Trent seriously and we may be uncertain how to say, with St. Paul, that we now stand in grace and can rejoice (rather than be anxious) in our hope. Take the Wesleys seriously and our sense of being still "on the way" may seem threatened, and anticipation rather than hope may be sufficient to shape the way we live.

We should note how deeply embedded in different understandings of grace are these differing assessments of the meaning of hope, and they take us back to issues discussed in section 2 above. When grace is understood chiefly as the pardoning promise of God, which makes Christ's righteousness the sinner's own, the signficance—before God—of what we do, of individual actions, almost inevitably recedes. In turn, then, our assurance for the future does not depend on what the character of our deeds may be, but, rather, on the promised mercy of God. When grace is understood chiefly as a power that moves us to become—through our deeds and through our traits of character—holy in God's eyes, assurance of future salvation might seem premature before the completion of this process of perfection.

At least for those of us who are not Thomists, it may seem that even the angelic doctor is pulled in several different directions. In IaIIae, q. 112, a. 5 of the *Summa* ("can a man know that he has grace?") Aquinas distinguishes three different ways in which one might know something: (1) through a special revelation, (2) through one's own cognitive capacities, and (3) by signs in one's life. To take them in reverse order, we may see signs in our life suggesting the working of God's grace, but that knowledge can never be perfect or complete. There are many things we may know through our own capacities, and even some things that we may know with certainty, but we cannot know with certainty things that are only in God's power. "In this sense no one can know that he has grace." (Here Aquinas refers to 1 Corinthians 4:4. "I am not aware of anything against myself, but I am not thereby acquitted. It is the Lord who judges me.") Finally, it is indeed possible that "by a special privilege God sometimes reveals this to people, so that the joy of complete security may begin in them even in this life, and so that they may carry out remarkable tasks more confidently and courageously and endure the evils of this present life; so it was said to Paul, *My grace is sufficient for you.*"

In St. Thomas's specific discussion of the virtue of hope, in IIaIIae, q. 17–22 of the *Summa*, his angle seems slightly different. In q. 18, a. 4 he says that hope involves the expectation of future salvation, and—replying to a possible objection to the effect that since hope of salvation "comes by way of grace and merits," we cannot be assured in this life that we have grace—he says: "Hope does not put its trust primarily in grace already received but in the divine omnipotence and mercy. . . . To anyone having faith, this omnipotence and mercy of God are certainties." We would, I think, be faithful to Aquinas's complexities if we said: Although grace has been bestowed by the Spirit, salvation remains future, and the way toward it must be traversed. Our question about certitude, then, asks whether Christians can be assured that they will, indeed, arrive at the promised destination.

Faith (understood as cognitive, as knowledge) does not enable us to know with certainty that we will be among the saved. But putting the matter that way is thinking of one's life in the third person, as an observer might—and no one can *live* that way. We can, on the other hand, say that the "omnipotence and mercy of God are certainties" when grasped in the first person by faith (understood not as knowledge but as trust). This is not to look at one's life from the outside; it is to turn to God and cling to his promises in confidence.

A useful comparison might be with the way the marriage vow must be taken. It cannot be simply a prediction about what may happen in the future, for any honest prediction must reckon with the fact that some marriages end in divorce. One cannot take the vow from that perspective of a third-person observer. I cannot say, "Yes, I will be faithful to you—unless, of course, I am one of those who turns out to fail in this commitment." Or, at any rate, if I say this, she is not likely to think I have taken the vow she wants from me. But I can meaningfully, even in the midst of living out that vow, hope that I will be faithful to it. That is, I can recognize that the way of faithfulness is arduous and strewn with temptations. Indeed, just as my spouse wants something more from me than a prediction of the future, even so she also wants to see in me this hope that sets its course with a clear recognition of the difficulties.

On this topic, as on those taken up in the two previous sections, the *Joint Declaration on the Doctrine of Justification* articulates substantial consensus. This comes out most clearly in a Roman Catholic affirmation whose cadence is not precisely that of Trent:

> With the Second Vatican Council, Catholics state: to have faith is to entrust oneself totally to God, who liberates us from the darkness of sin and death and awakens us to eternal life. In this sense, one cannot believe in God and at the same time consider the divine promise untrustworthy. No one may doubt God's mercy and Christ's merit. Every person, however, may be concerned about his salvation when he looks upon his own weaknesses and shortcomings. Recognizing his own failures,

however, the believer may yet be certain that God intends his salvation (4.6, 36).

If this is the kind of assurance with which Christians, shaped by grace, live toward the future God has promised, we might ask, finally and all too briefly, what difference it makes for the contours of our life.

One of the most influential streams of modern moral philosophy, and of much everyday moral reflection, has been what moral theorists call "consequentialism." This view holds that it is our responsibility to determine and seek to achieve the best overall state of affairs in all that we do. This suggests, however, a kind of presumption about our control of the future that sits uneasily in a life shaped by hope, whose assurance rests not in our mastery but in God's promises.

In the first section above, I explored briefly the analogy of the story, focusing on the author's role in working out the plot even in the face of "recalcitrant" characters (of his own creation). Now we can focus for a moment on the characters and on what it would mean to think of themselves as characters in a drama written by the divine author. They know the part given them, and each must play his part in his own way, with his own particular flair and interpretation. But none of the characters is the dramatist or director, and none of them knows how the plot is satisfactorily to be worked out. That is essentially our situation. C. S. Lewis put the metaphor this way:

> We do not know the play. We do not even know whether we are in Act I or Act V. We do not know who are the major and who the minor characters. The Author knows. . . . That it has a meaning we may be sure, but we cannot see it. When it is over, we may be told. We are led to expect that the Author will have something to say to each of us on the part that each of us has played. The playing it well is what matters infinitely.[40]

This is quite a different picture of the moral life from imagining ourselves responsible for achieving the best state of affairs possible. Christians are under authority, called to act faithfully within the limits of history, even when it is not apparent that such faithfulness leads in the direction of the greatest good overall.

There is no way to live such a life except in hope that the God revealed in Jesus will complete what remains incomplete in our own achievements, and such hope—a hope that goes well beyond any empirical evidence—must be the gift of God's grace. Indeed, we may well say with Barth that what "derives and proceeds" from our own capacities alone, however noble it may sometimes be, "can never be Christian faith, nor Christian love, nor Christian hope."[41] On the contrary, if the division within our being is to be overcome and our loves rightly ordered, if faith in God's favor toward us is to renew and energize our lives in habits of virtue, and if genuine hope is to free us for both love and faithfulness—if all that is to happen in human lives, we must credit the mystery of divine grace so powerfully gestured at in a hymn of Bianco da Siena:

> And so the yearning strong,
> With which the soul will long,
> Shall far outpass the pow'r of human telling;
> No soul shall guess his grace
> Till it become the place
> Wherein the Holy Spirit makes his dwelling.

Notes

1. An earlier version of this chapter, under the title "Divine Grace and Ethics," appeared as chapter 5 (pp. 74–89) of Gilbert Meilaender and William Werpehowski (eds.), *The Oxford Handbook of Theological Ethics* (Oxford: Oxford University Press, 2005).

2. Hans Urs von Balthasar, *The Theology of Karl Barth* (New York: Doubleday Anchor, 1972), pp. 7–8.

3. St. Augustine, *Confessions*, translated by Rex Warner (New York: Mentor Books, 1963), 8.5. Future citations will be given in parentheses within the body of the text.

4. Robert Merrihew Adams, *Finite and Infinite* (Oxford: Oxford University Press, 1999), p. 224.

5. Adams, p. 224.

6. *Luther's Works*, vol. 33 (Philadelphia: Fortress Press, 1972), pp. 65–66.

7. Ibid., p. 67.

8. St. Augustine, *City of God*, translated by Henry Bettenson (New York: Penguin Books, 1984), 5.10. Future citations will be given in parentheses within the body of the text.

9. Dorothy L. Sayers, *The Mind of the Maker* (San Francisco: Harper & Row, 1979), p. 67.

10. Ibid.

11. Ibid., pp. 69–70.

12. Ibid., p. 75.

13. Reinhold Niebuhr, *The Nature and Destiny of Man*, vol. 2 (New York: Charles Scribner's Sons, 1964), p. 190.

14. Ibid., p. 196.

15. H. J. Schroeder, O.P. (trans.), *Canons and Decrees of the Council of Trent* (St. Louis: B. Herder, 1941), p. 23.

16. The Lutheran World Federation and the Roman Catholic Church, *Joint Declaration on the Doctrine of Justification* (Grand Rapids: Eerdmans, 2000), 4.4, 29. Futher citations will be given in parentheses within the body of the text.

17. Niebuhr, p. 141.

18. Anthony N. S. Lane, *Justification by Faith in Catholic-Protestant Dialogue* (London and New York: T & T Clark, 2002), p. 176.

19. Richard J. Mouw, *He Shines in All That's Fair: Culture and Common Grace* (Grand Rapids: Eerdmans, 2001), p. 9.

20. John Calvin, *Institutes of the Christian Religion* (Philadelphia: Westminster Press, 1960), II,14.

21. Mouw, p. 43.

22. Anders Nygren, *Agape and Eros* (London: SPCK, 1953), p. 455.

23. Ibid., p. 129.

24. Kenneth E. Kirk, *The Vision of God* (London: Longmans, Green, 1932).

25. St. Augustine, "On the Spirit and the Letter," in Whitney J. Oates (ed.), *The Basic Writings of Saint Augustine* (New York: Random House, 1948), p. 471.

26. Ibid., p. 494.

27. Ibid., p. 487.

28. Karl Rahner, "Some Implications of the Scholastic Concept of Uncreated Grace," in *Theological Investigations*, vol. 1 (Baltimore: Helicon Press, 1965), p. 322.

29. Thomas F. O'Meara, O.P., "Virtues in the Theology of Thomas Aquinas," *Theological Studies*, 58 (June 1997), p. 262.

30. Theo Kobusch, "Grace (IaIIae, qq. 109–114)," in Stephen J. Pope (ed.), *The Ethics of Aquinas* (Washington, D.C.: Georgetown University Press, 2002), p. 212.

31. *Luther's Works*, vol. 32 (Philadelphia: Fortress Press, 1958), p. 229.

32. For the language of "again and again" and "more and more," see George Hunsinger, *Disruptive Grace: Studies in the Theology of Karl Barth* (Grand Rapids: Eerdmans, 2000), pp. 299–300.

33. Niebuhr, pp. 124, 107.

34. Ibid., p. 125.

35. Hunsinger, p. 304.

36. Edward Yarnold, "*Duplex iustitia:* The Sixteenth Century and the Twentieth," in G. R. Evans (ed.), *Christian Authority: Essays in Honour of Henry Chadwick* (Oxford: Clarendon Press, 1988), pp. 204–23.

37. Lane, p. 234.

38. Schroeder, p. 35.

39. Frank Whaling (ed.), *John and Charles Wesley: Selected Prayers, Hymns, Journal Notes, Sermons, Letters and Treatises* (New York: Paulist Press, 1981), p. 107.

40. C. S. Lewis, *The World's Last Night and Other Essays* (New York: Harcourt Brace Jovanovich, 1960), pp. 105–6.

41. Karl Barth, *Church Dogmatics*, IV/3.2 (Edinburgh: T & T Clark, 1962), p. 939.

PART TWO

Freedom
for God's Call

4

Freedom for the
Command of God:
Thinking with Johannes[1]

L uther famously summarized Christian life in terms of a
    twofold freedom, namely, that (1) a Christian is a per-
    fectly free lord of all, subject to none; and (2) a Christian
is a perfectly dutiful servant of all, subject to all. I aim to try
to understand this conception of freedom—both the way in
which it sets the believer free from moral law and the way it
reclaims that same moral law—not by returning to Luther but
via a reading of Kierkegaard's *Fear and Trembling*.[2] In listening
to the voice of Kierkegaard's pseudonym, Johannes *de silentio*,
I myself hear a Lutheran voice. A work as elusive and allusive
as *Fear and Trembling* can, of course, be read in more than one
way—and has been. Other, far better, Kierkegaard scholars
will surely "go further" than I in their understanding of *Fear
and Trembling*, though in Johannes's own terms, of course, to
"go further" is a very ambiguous achievement indeed.

Johannes puzzles over Abraham's willingness to sacrifice Isaac
not because he is puzzled about whether one might be permitted to

sacrifice one's child but because he finds the life of faith constantly baffling. Perhaps because it is so baffling, few are content simply to stand before God on that basis. "Today nobody will stop with faith," Johannes says in his Preface, "they all go further" (42).

Abraham is, according to Johannes, a knight of faith. To understand what it means that Abraham has faith we must pay attention to the contrasts that Johannes provides. In particular, Abraham is not a tragic hero—such as Agamemnon, Jephthah, or Brutus. They too make great sacrifices. They might even be said to renounce their greatest earthly loves. But they do it (or so one might, at least, argue) for good moral reason, for the good of the larger community. If asked to justify their awful deeds, each can make reply, can give a reason that might serve as his justification.

To see that is also to understand why Abraham must keep silent, why he cannot explain to Isaac or anyone else what he does. No doubt more can be said about his silence, but there is at least this: The necessity for silence does not mean that Abraham could not recount to us what is happening. He could—every bit as much as Johannes can. Abraham must be silent for a different reason—because he can offer no ethical warrant for what he does. He can offer no moral reason of the sort the tragic hero gives as his justification.

Why not? Why could not Abraham say, "Look, God commanded me to sacrifice my son"? But that can serve as justification only if Abraham means, "Whenever God commands anyone to do a certain deed, that person ought to do it." That is, God's command serves as Abraham's justification only if Abraham turns it into a universal principle: "Everyone should always obey God's commands." But then Abraham is not responding directly and immediately to God. He is obeying God *because* he has a moral principle that tells him to. The ethical is higher than the religious, higher than the God-relation. Then Abraham is responding to God as "him" (the one whose commands ought to be obeyed) rather than as "you." Hence, if Abraham really wants to respond directly to God, to trust God, he cannot justify himself in the way a tragic hero can. He must remain silent.

If Abraham is not a tragic hero, neither is he merely a knight of infinite resignation. To be sure, he does make the movement of infinite resignation—that is, he gives up at God's command the son he loves dearly, resigning himself to Isaac's loss. But he also does what Johannes calls believing that he will get Isaac back in this life. Abraham "believed on the strength of the absurd" (65). He makes the second movement, which takes one beyond infinite resignation to faith. In order to understand Abraham (or, at least, to understand Johannes), therefore, we must make sense of how in everyday life one might have to renounce the finite good, relate absolutely to God, and then "on the strength of the absurd," believe that one will receive it back again.

An example: Suppose I fall in love with a woman and would like to marry her, but my friends tell me she doesn't really love me. Before making so important a commitment, I want to be certain that she does. I don't want to end up looking like a fool—the butt of my friends' jokes. So I test her, I check up on her, perhaps I even hire a private investigator to track her movements. Can this provide the certainty I desire? She might, after all, be outsmarting me at every turn. No evidence will provide the kind of certainty I need here.

So I could simply give her up. Unable to be certain of her love, I could make the movement of infinite resignation. For I cannot relate to her in love and trust through what we might call the universal—through the sorts of reasons, evidence, and proof that my friends or anyone else can understand. No reasons of that sort could really justify the kind of commitment I have wished to make. So, though still loving her, I give her up.

That could end the story, but it need not. I have given her up in the sense that I have given up any notion that our bond can be justified on the basis of evidence open for universal inspection by anyone and everyone. There can never be airtight reasons of that sort to justify my commitment. Hence, I relinquish that kind of certainty. But suppose that I now make a second move and decide to trust her. This second movement is not based on any evidence to which all of us might nod in assent. My trust is simply that—trust. We might even say that it is based "on the strength of the absurd."

In this way, I get her back. But our relation is no longer "mediated," as Johannes likes to say. It is not mediated by any sort of evidence, universally available, that would make my commitment reasonable and justifiable. Our relationship is "immediate"—a purely personal bond of commitment. I no longer think of her in the third person—as in, "she is a trustworthy woman, worthy of love." I address her as "you"—as in, "I love you." To some, of course, it might seem absurd to make such a commitment without good evidence to offer by way of justification. But, in fact, there isn't any other way to enter into such a personal bond. Faith always precedes the evidence. We can give up such personal bonds if we wish, but we cannot enter them on any basis other than faith. Thus, I give her up in the sense that I renounce proof of her trustworthiness. And I get her back, based on the absurd movement of faith.

Such an example is very much in the spirit of Johannes. The knight of faith may lead what is—to our eye—an ordinary existence; for "the movement of faith must be made continually on the strength of the absurd, though in such a way, be it noted, that one does not lose finitude but gains it all of a piece" (67). In every moment—moment by moment—he makes the double movement. "He drains in infinite resignation the deep sorrow of existence," renouncing whatever is most precious to him and knowing that he cannot finally justify his commitment, and he then receives everything back on the strength of the absurd. He manages "to express the sublime in the pedestrian absolutely," living joyfully in every moment (70).

This double movement applies not only to the beloved but also to the moral law. The knight of infinite resignation plays it safe and gets in return a kind of security. Having given up the one he loves, he nevertheless knows that he has done so for good reason. He has not lost the greater good, has not been fooled—as all can clearly see. By contrast, the knight of faith gets not security but "is kept in constant tension" (106). Likewise with the moral law. Abraham loves Isaac with all his soul, yet renounces him. He does not say as does the tragic hero, "I wish I could save Isaac, but duty calls me to sacrifice him." Rather, he says, "I wish I could save Isaac, and duty requires me to save him—but I will sacrifice him at God's command, believing on the strength of the absurd that I shall have him back." He has lost not only his son but also the security that comes from knowing one does one's duty. From the ethical point of view, Abraham is being *tempted* to do what is universally forbidden. From the religious point of view, Abraham is being *tested*—that is, tempted to adhere to the universal moral rule rather than to obey God's command.

In order, therefore, to live in the immediacy of personal relationship with God, "in absolute relation to the absolute" (85), we must renounce any attempt to relate to God on the basis of the moral law—Johannes's teleological suspension of the ethical. A tragic hero such as Agamemnon gives up one lower expression of the ethical (love for his daughter), permitting the ethical to find its telos in a higher expression (love for the community). "But the person [the knight of faith] who gives up the universal [moral law and duty] to grasp something still higher that is not the universal, what does he do" (89)? How can one give up the universal to grasp something still higher? What could be higher than the universal?

Answer: the God who is personal and particular, concrete rather than abstract. The personal is higher than the universal, and within a logic of personal relations trust must always precede and outrun proof or reasonableness or justification. But how then does one who has teleologically suspended the ethical live? Must he live as a sinner? "He exists as the particular in opposition to the universal. Does this mean he sins? For this [living as the particular in opposition to the universal] is the form of sin looked at ideally. . . . Then how did Abraham exist? He had faith" (90). He lives by faith—absolutely related to the absolute.

And then he gets the finite back. All of it—including the moral law. This we must understand, lest we turn Johannes into that pseudo-Lutheran who can speak only of freedom and who does not really make the second movement in its full extent.

Abraham does not just relinquish his son. He gives up as well the moral norms governing the relation of fathers to sons. Those norms are universal. Fathers ought to love their sons. Fathers ought not kill their sons (unless for the tragic hero some greater good requires it). Were Abraham to try to base his relation with God on such norms—to live in "mediated" relation to God—he could always justify his actions. In that

case, to learn his moral duties would be to know what he must
do to please God. Once he knew his moral duties, however,
God would scarcely be needed, would become a redundant
"invisible, vanishing point" (96). But, instead, Abraham relin-
quishes any attempt to relate to God on the basis of morality.
He "determines his relation to the universal through his relation to the absolute, not his relation to the absolute through his
relation to the universal" (97–98).

Nevertheless, the knight of faith does still have a relation to
the universal, determined through his relation to God. Having
made the first movement and resigned himself to the loss of the
finite, including the loss of any way to justify himself on the basis
of universal moral law—when, then, he makes the second movement and believes that he will receive the finite back, he does.
He gets back the moral law as the command of God—relating
to the universal through his relation to the absolute.

Recall my earlier example: When, on the strength of the absurd, I promise lifelong fidelity to the woman I love and marry her
after renouncing any hope of making such a commitment seem
reasonable and justified, I receive her back—though not as one
for whose trustworthiness I can offer persuasive evidence. Hence,
our relationship is altered and transformed. It is a personal bond,
based on trust, not a relation justified by reasonable evidence.
The same is true when the knight of faith receives back the moral
law. The norms themselves do not change, but now they are the
command of the living God, who may command anew at any
moment. The knight of faith receives the law not as a permanent
possession in the keeping of which he can find security, but,
rather, moment by moment from the hand of God.

In this sense, the moral law is relativized—not that *we* may
be free, but that *God* may be. For it is not the law or duty that
binds us, but God, to whom we listen anew in every moment.
Of course, as Johannes himself clearly realizes, so to honor the
freedom of God might be thought to mean that, in principle, God
could command anything—torture of the innocent, rape, etc.
There are moments when Johannes seems too ready to acquiesce
in this, inclining briefly toward that sort of pseudo-Lutheran
who, alas, can be very hard to distinguish from a gnostic. Thus,

for example, Johannes says at one point that, after the double movement has been made, the ethical "gets a quite different expression, the paradoxical expression, so that, e.g., love of God can cause the knight of faith to give his love of his neighbour the opposite expression to that which is his duty ethically speaking" (98). The God who might command anything, a god hard to distinguish from Satan, would soar so high above this created world's discernible order and structure as to be another power altogether from the One who created all things through his Word and has been made known in the face of Jesus.

I do not think that is where Johannes is finally heading. Rather, what we should learn from the knight of faith—who is far more concerned about God's freedom than his own—is that the ethical life, the life of duty, is a vocation, to which we are called anew day by day. The call comes first, the unmediated relation to God, and the moral life flows out of that relation as God commands us afresh in every moment. Thus, the Christian who is a perfectly free lord of all, subject to none, is, in fact, subject to One. And the Christian who is a perfectly dutiful servant of all, subject to all, subjects himself not to duty but to the living God, who calls us to serve the neighbor. Our freedom from the moral law understood as universally binding duty is freedom for the commanding God who gives us that moral law day by day.

The moral life, then, is not our possession, but the gift of God, whose command is our calling. This should help us understand what is wrong with all those who, as Johannes complains in his Preface, keep wanting to "go further" than faith. And it should help us understand why he says in the Epilogue that every generation must begin afresh, that "no generation has learned from another how to love, no generation can begin other than at the beginning" (145). The way of life that is faith, as an immediate relation to God for which no conclusive argument can be given, is not a possession that anyone can hand on to others. We cannot even hand it on without fail to our children; it just cannot be mediated. Hence, it is not simply the starting point from which the moral life begins, but is a journey that regularly returns to its starting point, constantly beginning again in relation to God. Whatever God may do in us, we ourselves can never "go further" than faith—only back to faith. And all this must be said not for the sake of human freedom but for the sake of God's freedom to call and command us.

This may also help to explain why *Fear and Trembling* is the convoluted, puzzling book that it is. If I have read the book at all rightly, it would probably be possible to set forth its—actually quite simple—thesis about the life of faith much more directly than Johannes does. I might even claim to have done that here.

But I have been writing "about" the life of faith. And that kind of talk can itself become a new form of mediation—coming between the reader and God, making the life of faith seem sensible and reasonable. But the aim is not chiefly that we should learn to think better "about" faith, but that we should make the movement "of" faith. These are quite different matters, as Johannes reminds us: "I for my part can indeed describe the movements of faith, but I cannot perform them. When learning how to make swimming movements, one can hang in a belt from the ceiling; one may be said to describe the movements all right but one isn't swimming; likewise I can describe the movements of faith but when I am thrown into the water, although I may be said to be swimming (for I'm not among the waders), I make other movements" (67).

Johannes's task is not therefore to persuade us, but to coax, puzzle, and bewilder us into making the life of faith of our own. As the point of the book is so simple, even so must its form be convoluted—lest we should think that we had somehow understood the life of faith, that it had just been passed on to us. Lest we should not be summoned out into that freedom of faith whereby God calls us to do as he commands.

Notes

1. An earlier version of this chapter was published, under the same title, in *Dialog*, 39 (Winter 2000), pp. 257–61.

2. Søren Kierkegaard, *Fear and Trembling: Dialectical Lyric by Johannes de silentio*. Translated by Alastair Hannay (New York: Penguin Books, 1985). Citations will be given by page number in parentheses within the body of the text.

5

Vocation as Permission[1]

Most of us, at least some of the time, are tempted to think that whatever is right for us to do must also be right for anyone else in similar circumstances—that is, that something like Kant's universalization requirement must apply to the whole of life. And, of course, there is a good (moral) reason why we might think this. We may fear that when we or others deny it, we are making excuses to protect a guilty conscience. Or we may see this requirement as a demand for fairness and as a check on and discipline for our self-regarding impulses.

Without, of course, in any way wanting to deny the claims of fairness, I do want to ask whether it is necessary to hold that, whenever I think I ought to act in a certain way, I am committed to thinking that all persons similarly situated should choose to act in the same way. I will offer several reasons for doubting such a claim. By contrast, my thesis, roughly stated, is that a universalization requirement can apply only to a certain restricted set of moral obligations—those which, to use Kant's language, constitute our duties of perfect obligation. This can for now be only a rough statement, because a consideration of certain complexities will require that this simple thesis undergo some modification later.

It may be helpful at the outset, though, to distinguish several different senses of a universalizability requirement. J. L. Mackie, for example, noted three different roles that universalization might play in our moral reasoning.[2] First, it might require straightforwardly that all merely numerical differences between one person and another should be deemed irrelevant. Thus, according to Mackie, the ascetic should not say, "I cannot allow myself such indulgences, but I do not condemn them in others."[3] But, of course, this first formulation would not prohibit a strong man from adopting and universalizing a principle endorsing rigorous competition and survival of the fittest. A second way to formulate a universalizability thesis—beyond the obvious preference of self involved in regarding numerical difference as morally relevant—is to require that we seek imaginatively to put ourselves in another's place. Thus, the strong man would ask himself what life would be like for the weak man in a rigorously competitive world, and whether he would want that life to be his. Finally, a third approach would require not only that we imagine ourselves in the other's place but also that we imagine that—while in his place—we share his preferences, values, and ideals. Thus, the strong man would not consider that, even in a harsh world, *he* prefers to be self-reliant. He would consider instead the preferences of the other person.

Only the first of these ways can with any plausibility be said to be a requirement built into the *logic* of moral language (and even that may not be the case). The third is clearly a substantive moral position and, indeed, one which, though perhaps useful for achieving political compromise in a pluralistic society, may be quite unsatisfactory as a fundamental moral stance. My discussion will for the most part be limited to the first and second ways.

I

Any adequate ethic must, I think, acknowledge that we have some moral responsibilities that oblige all persons similarly situated. But if we characterize the whole of morality in those terms, we destroy any possibility of choosing the sort of person we will be, of determining our character through the choices we freely make. There are many important human goods that we might foster in life—goods as diverse as close personal friendships, communion with nature, self-sacrificing service of others, cultivation and creation of beauty, worship of God, and so forth. It seems true to say of these goods (1) that they are incommensurable; and (2) that any of us might say to himself and to others when choosing a way of life: "This is what I ought to do; nothing else would be right for me." It is the ineradicable use of moral language in such first-person contexts that a universalizability *requirement* fails to make space for.[4]

Of such a life-determination we may want to use the language of decision ("I am determining my being") or of discovery ("I am finding out something about myself"). The fact that we may consider it our vocation, our calling, indicates that it may be and often is regarded as a discovery, not merely a decision. Perhaps either sort of language is appropriate; for it may be that here discovery and decision are inseparable. Those who want to require universalizability throughout the whole of the moral life must either deprive us of the words "ought" and "right" in such contexts or deprive us of the freedom to determine our character in a way of life.

"One of the marks of a certain type of bad man," C. S. Lewis once wrote, "is that he cannot give up a thing himself without wanting everyone else to give it up."[5] To be such a bad person is what universalizability requires of us. We may recall that at even the first stage of the universalizing process Mackie did not want to permit the ascetic to say, "I cannot allow myself such indulgences, but I do not condemn them in others."

To eliminate such a possibility from the moral life would deprive us of the freedom to determine our way of life in such a way as to consider it peculiarly *ours*. Hence, accounts that shape the whole of moral reasoning in accord with a universalizability requirement (or an "original position" or "ideal observer") force us "to regard our life as would an observer."[6] I cannot think that I *ought* to forego meat twice a week because there are many hungry people in the world or because it is a useful discipline without committing myself to the belief that all of us who are not starving (except perhaps children, pregnant women, and those with certain health problems) ought to do likewise. There are countless decisions like this which, when we make them, shape our character and vocation and determine the manner in which our life will relate to others. To deprive us of the ability to use "ought"-language concerning those choices not only flies in the face of ordinary language but also removes from morality's realm many of the most important decisions people ever make. And to permit "ought"-language here but require that it be universalized does not do justice to the place of self-determination in human life.

Although extreme cases are not necessarily the best for making a point, it may be instructive to consider the case of Captain Oates, who walked out of his tent to die in the Antarctic (lest his disability should keep his fellow adventurers from returning safely). W. D. Hudson maintains that if Oates had said to himself, "I ought to walk away," he would have been committed to requiring the same of all similarly situated persons. "Would Oates have rejected that implication? I doubt it. Surely a man in his position, acting as he did, we presume from a sense of duty, would think that anyone in the same position who failed so to act would be blameworthy."[7]

Perhaps—though I am uncertain even about this—Oates (were he to wax philosophical at such a moment) would think that any person similarly situated, who held the set of ideals which he himself held, ordered and balanced those ideals in the same way, and had committed himself to the same way of life, would also be committed to walking out of the tent. But to put it that way is at once to see that Hudson's claim must read into "similarly situated" the character and vocation of the particular person who is Captain Oates. Apart from the legitimate worry that doing so may trivialize the universalizability requirement, we might wonder whether Oates could really imagine others to have committed themselves to the same way of life while still calling it *his* life.

Even if we could make sense of such a universal requirement, it would still be quite different from the sort of duty that is universalizable in any strong sense. Suppose, for example, Captain Oates had decided that, in order to make his food supplies last longer, he should take his companions by surprise and kill them. We would, I believe, condemn such an act in the case of Captain Oates and anyone else who shared his ideals. But, more important, we would condemn anyone at all—whatever his ideals—who ventured to take this way out of that predicament. We would feel no need to inquire about his ideals or the way of life he had chosen before rendering moral judgment. To see that is to see the sphere in which universalizable duties make sense.

Certain fundamental moral obligations are indeed universalizable, but the ways in which we exercise our beneficence toward others (usually) are not. Indeed, I suspect that if we thought Oates's act should be required of anyone similarly situated, we would not really think it told us much about his character, about the man Oates was. It could not have such meaning for us if we thought, as Hudson does, that Oates himself would assume that anyone else in his position would be blameworthy for not doing the same.

Thus, I make no claim that all choices concerning what we ought to do are free from the requirements of universalization. There are duties which bind all of us and which we are free to omit only at our moral peril. We may account for these in different ways: with Kant (duties of perfect obligation), with Philippa Foot (negative duties), with Germain Grisez (basic human goods against which one may not directly turn), with H. L. A. Hart (minimum content of natural law), or with Yahweh (the Decalog). What we ought not do, however, is extend the claim of universalizability beyond these duties to the whole of the moral life.

It is worth noting that there is a connection between what is claimed to be a purely logical requirement of universalization and the substantive requirement of utilitarianism (universal and impartial benevolence). Both are imperialistic. The utilitarian, believing all human goods to be commensurable, thinks that (at least in principle) we can prescribe how each of us ought to exercise his or her benevolence. On this theory, benevolence is no longer an imperfect obligation, binding on us all in different (and freely chosen) ways. Instead, the course my benevolence ought to take is strictly determined. Anyone similarly situated ought to be benevolent in exactly the same way. At this point the requirement of universalizability merges with universal and impartial benevolence, and the realm of the "permitted" is obliterated, destroying genuine freedom in vocation.

II

Thus far I have simply suggested that, though some moral obligations are universalizable, they by no means constitute the totality of the moral life. Having done our duty in the limited sense of meeting those obligations, there remain for each of us countless decisions about who and what we shall be and how we shall aid others—decisions which cannot be universalized, though we might well use the moral ought in speaking of them. Universalizable moral duties remain fundamental in the sense that one ought not, I think, choose a vocation that requires their systematic violation. We should permit them that much imperialism, but no more.

Now, however, we must complicate this thesis a bit.[8] We have to grant that the Kantian language, which characterizes beneficence as a duty of imperfect obligation, may be misleading. Consider the following case: I am starting my usual after-dinner stroll during which I make it a point to think of nothing significant. As I walk out to the street I notice the neighbor child playing in the street where she may possibly be injured by one of the passing cars that often speed down our street. It will take relatively little effort for me to take the child over to her parents, who are planting flowers along the side of their house. To do so would, I suppose, be characterized as a beneficent act. To fail to do so would not precisely be to inflict harm on the child. Yet I imagine we would think that anyone in my situation ought to remove the child from the dangerous place where she is playing. The child's need is relatively great; my loss if I help her, relatively small.

This is an obligation which seems universalizable even though it requires more than merely refraining from inflicting harm. It requires that one bring aid. Hence, it was not incorrect of Luther to write, in explanation of the commandant that forbids killing, "We should fear and love God that we may not hurt nor harm our neighbor in his body, but help and befriend him in every bodily need." There are, however, limits to what we can be morally required to do in bringing aid (whereas there are, in my view, no limits on the requirement that we refrain from doing certain evils). If, instead of finding the neighbor child playing in the street, I see her drowning in the ocean, and if furthermore I cannot myself swim, I do not think I am morally required to try to save her. Even so, if when I catch a glimpse of her terrified eyes as her head bobs up, I say to myself, "I ought to give it a try," that is a correct use of moral language. It announces or expresses the person I am or will be. But that moral language cannot be universalized.

What distinguishes these cases? We might suggest at first that they are distinguished by the different degree of burden I must bear and the risk I must run. It is, after all, likely to cost me far more to launch out in the ocean than it will to interrupt briefly my evening stroll. And there is surely something to this explanation. It is part of the reason Christians have often claimed that only grace could elicit from a person like me a decision to brave the waves and try to save the child; for such a decision would require a degree of self-forgetfulness not naturally to be expected (or required) of us.

But I do not think that the burden or cost to the agent can be the decisive factor. Consider another case. Suppose others judge me capable of doing great benefit as a physician. Suppose also that I have made no commitments which would make it impossible for me to undertake the necessary training, that I know myself capable of it, feel reasonably sure that I would not be unhappy as a doctor, believe there is a great need for doctors, and would not have to make any overwhelming sacrifice to become one. Suppose also, however, that what I really want to do, what I would find most satisfying, is running a catering service for elite country clubs. Should I be subject to moral censure if I decide that others, perhaps even those less suited for the task, will have to be physicians while I run my catering service? I think not; for this is simply one of those choices which goes beyond the moral law and determines one's being. As long as, in making it, I do not violate any of my fundamental moral duties, I cannot be blamed.

This is an instance where the question of cost or burden borne by the agent does not seem to be a crucial factor. Rather, what seems to be important is what a decision does to one's character. If, when the little girl is playing in the street where cars speed by, I blithely continue my stroll, I help to make myself a person who is indifferent to the obvious needs of other human beings. If her parents ask me why I did not move her when I saw her in the street and I answer that I thought perhaps someone else might, that is not likely to seem a very good answer. If, on the other hand, my very sick neighbor catches me in a spare moment when I am not catering at the country club and says, "You might have helped me had you become a doctor," I am entitled to respond, as Charles Fried suggests, "No more than countless other persons."[9] The little girl playing in the street is particularized; to ignore her need is to shape my character in important ways. It begins to make of me the sort of person who will not be beneficent at all. The same is not true of the decision to cater at country clubs. That vocational choice tells us nothing about whether we might expect me to respond with help for (at least some) human beings in need, even to respond at great cost to myself. For that choice involves no rejection of the duty to be beneficent.

Thus, the crucial factor is not merely the cost or burden borne by the agent. Relevant also—and, I think, more important—is the effect on the character of the agent, the degree to which a particular decision will necessarily help to create a person indifferent to human need. As long as our vocational decisions do not shape our character in that way, we are free—free to make of ourselves what we will, free of the imperialism of any universalization requirement.

III

In Deuteronomy 7 (6–8a) the reason (if we can call it that) for Israel's election is given as follows:

> For you are a people holy to the LORD your God; the LORD your God has chosen you to be a people for his own possession, out of all the peoples that are on the face of the earth. It was not because you were more in number than any other people that the LORD set his love upon you and chose you, for you were the fewest of all peoples; but it is because the LORD loves you.

In the Bible terms such as "grace" and "mercy" are terms of particular, personal relationships, for which no more universal rationale can be given. This is quite different from the sense we give to "mercy"—as when, for example, we say that it ought to temper justice.[10] God's mercy rests upon Israel for no reason—beyond the simple fact that it does. Similarly with Jesus's parable (Matt. 20:1–16) of the laborers in the vineyard. Some work many hours, enduring the heat of the day; others begin only near the very end of the workday. Yet all receive the same wage. This is not injustice to those who worked longest (or so the owner of the vineyard claims) but generosity and mercy toward those who came last.

An ethic which aims for the kind of universality I have been questioning here may, then, find itself judging even the holiness of God. As Donald Mackinnon once wrote with respect to Kant's ethic: "There is a kind of arrogance here, and also more than a hint of the clear subordination of what is personal—namely God and men and their relation to Him—to something which is formal and universal, even in a special sense abstract—namely the law of reason."[11] My concern here, though, is not with judging the holiness of God but with whether such personal, particularized concern can be a justifiable feature of our actions toward each other.

Even if God can always be trusted when showing this kind of particularized, personal mercy, we probably cannot. That is sufficient reason for thinking that some of our basic duties must be subject to the requirement of universalization. It represents a drive for fairness, and it disciplines our self-regarding impulses. To apply this to the whole of life is, however, as Mackinnon hints, a kind of pretension. We do not, like God, have unlimited responsibilities that are universal in scope. We are tied to particular people in particular times and places—and we may wish to spend ourselves especially in their behalf and, even, think we ought to. If we are asked why they should be preferred to the countless other people living (and still to be born), we are not likely to find an answer better than Moses's "because the LORD loves you." This does not mean that such an answer justifies any conduct at all. The basic duties limit the ways and the degree to which we may prefer the needs of certain people. But within the discretionary space they leave—within that realm of the permitted—we are free.

Advocates of universalization cannot deny what all of us know: that "arbitrarily" focused, personalized and particularized, concern adds much of great importance to human life. They are therefore likely to defend preferential attention on grounds something like Sidgwick's suggestion that "each person is for the most part, from limitations either of power or knowledge, not in a position to do much good to more than a very small number of persons; it therefore seems, on this ground alone, desirable that his chief benevolent impulses should be correspondingly limited."[12] Sidgwick here has his hand on the right idea, our calling to a place and people, but he misunderstands its significance. It is as if, being located, we were to give a grudging acquiescence to this fact while doing all we can to blunt its significance for human life. What is needed, instead, is a glad affirmation of the place and the tasks we have been given—an affirmation that we are creatures rather than Creator and that, therefore, our responsibilities are real but limited.

IV

It may be suggested that, in terms of the tradition of Christian ethics, I have been asserting the importance of the traditional

Roman Catholic distinction between a lower realm of duty (commands) and a higher standard of perfection (counsels). While there would be some truth to that suggestion, an important difference must be noted. There is, on the view I have been defending, no particular vocation that is saintly or closer to perfection. Or, to put it differently, all ways of life that do not in themselves violate the fundamental duties we owe all human beings are ways that saints may choose to live.

This does not mean, however, that God will necessarily permit us to rest content with the decisions we have made or the way of life that seems choiceworthy to us. For God remains free to summon us from the location where he has placed us. Even then, however, that call will always be personal and particular.

Notes

1. This chapter was first published under the descriptive, if somewhat ungainly, title, "Is What Is Right for Me Right for All Persons Similarly Situated?" in *The Journal of Religious Ethics*, 8 (1980), pp. 125–34.

2. J. L. Mackie, *Ethics: Inventing Right and Wrong* (New York: Penguin Books, 1977), pp. 83–102.

3. Ibid., p. 84.

4. It seems clear to me that we do indeed speak this way, and that this "ought" can only be characterized as a moral one. In *The Nature of Morality* (New York: Oxford University Press, 1977) Gilbert Harman distinguishes four senses of "ought." They are (1) an ought of expectation (Oscar ought to be here by now); (2) an ought of evaluation (there ought to be more time for baseball in life); (3) an ought of reasons (the thief ought to wear gloves); and (4) the moral ought. I do not see how statements of the sort I am discussing, statements which we often utter, can be anything other than the moral ought.

5. C. S. Lewis, *Mere Christianity* (New York: Macmillan, 1960), p. 62.

6. Stanley Hauerwas and David Burrell, "From System to Story: An Alternative Pattern for Rationality in Ethics," in H. Tristram Engelhardt and Daniel Callahan (eds.), *Knowledge, Value and Belief* (Hastings-on-Hudson, NY: The Hastings Center, 1977), p. 122.

7. W. D. Hudson, *Modern Moral Philosophy* (Garden City, NY: Doubleday Anchor, 1970), p. 221.

8. Some of the examples and arguments in the following paragraphs, though certainly not the conclusions, were put to me many years ago by David Little.

9. Charles Fried, *Right and Wrong* (Cambridge: Harvard University Press, 1978), p. 38.

10. Oliver O'Donovan, *Measure for Measure: Justice in Punishment and the Sentence of Death*, Grove Booklets on Ethics, no. 19 (1977), pp. 14–15.

11. D. M. Mackinnon, *A Study in Ethical Theory* (London: Adam & Charles Black, 1957), p. 104.

12. Henry Sidgwick, *The Methods of Ethics* (London: Macmillan, 1907), p. 434.

6

————————

The Divine Summons:
The Infinite Horizon
of Vocation[1]

I have learned over the years that students, wearily carrying out a paper-writing assignment, often have recourse to the dictionary. Assigned to write on a specific topic, they will begin with a dictionary definition. Let it never be said that I have learned nothing from reading their papers all these years. Look up the word "vocation" in a dictionary, and you will find that the first two meanings given will be something like the following: (1) "a summons or strong inclination to a particular state or course of action: *esp*: a divine call to the religious life"; and (2) "the work in which a person is regularly employed: *occupation*."

It was in part the genius, and in part the danger, of the Reformations of the sixteenth century that they tended to collapse the first of these into the second. One's vocation became simply one's work. To be sure, for the Reformers this was a wider concept than what we have come to mean by work—which is, roughly, a job for the doing of which one is paid, a way to make a living. For example, familial responsibilities, though they do not belong to the sphere of work, were clearly understood by the Reformers to be part of one's vocation. Hence, a man could be very conscientious in the duties of his occupation and still fail terribly in his calling as a father. Even granting such qualifications, however, it is true to say that for the Reformers vocation came to be associated with the responsibilities of everyday life, rather than with a divine summons to do something extraordinary. To that sanctification of everyday work—and to the dangers of such sanctification—I will return in a little while. It is one of the tensions built into our concept of vocation.

Even if we connect vocation not only with work but also with the domestic and familial responsibilities so essential to life, there may be other duties that call us as well. When Ken Burns produced his much-acclaimed series of public television shows on the Civil War, one of the most powerful moments for many listeners was the reading of a letter written by Major Sullivan Ballou of the Second Rhode Island regiment of the Union Army to his wife, Sarah. Believing that his regiment would engage in battle within a few days, and reckoning with the fact that he might not return alive to her or to his sons, he wrote to Sarah, using quite naturally the language of vocation: "I have sought most closely and diligently, and often in my breast, for a wrong motive in thus hazarding the happiness of those I loved and could not find one. A pure love of my Country and the principles I have often advocated before the people, and 'the name of honor that I love more than I fear death' have called upon me, and I have obeyed." In such an instance we may find it harder to say whether we are still talking about the duties of everyday life, or whether a sense of vocation is here associated with something more heroic and extraordinary. In any case, this example begins to push us in the direction of the first—and deeper—tension I want to explore.

Students writing their papers tend to look simply at the several dictionary definitions of a word, but an unusually diligent student might also find ways to make use of the etymological information supplied in a dictionary entry. In the instance of the word "vocation," this is not very complicated. Our English word has its root in the Latin *vocare*—to call or to summon. A vocation is a calling—which implies a Caller. It is a summons. Taking this seriously will, I think, draw us into reflection upon a disturbing problem built into the idea of vocation. It reminds us also that—however often the concept of vocation has been connected especially to the Reformers, Luther and Calvin—the concept also has other important roots in Western culture.

It is, after all, Aeneas, depicted by Vergil as the destined founder of Rome, who says, in Robert Fitzgerald's translation: "I am the man / Whom heaven calls" (*ego poscor Olympo*). The *Aeneid* is, among other things, a poem about vocation. In their book *Heroism and the Christian Life*, Brian Hook and Russell Reno have noted how Vergil's poem, certainly one of the formative epics of our culture, compels us to ponder what is the deepest problem in the idea of a vocation—namely, whether obedience to a divine summons diminishes or enhances the one who has been called. So I begin there.

I

Of the *Aeneid* C. S. Lewis once wrote that no one "who has once read it with full perception remains an adolescent." What he had in mind was the Vergilian sense of vocation, which distinguishes the *Aeneid* from Homer's equally great epic, the *Iliad*. Homer's subject is not really the great contest between Greeks and Trojans; it is the personal story of Achilles' refusal to fight and of the events that bring him, finally, to change his mind. It is a story about the personal glory and honor of a heroic figure, and in such a story there may be fate but not vocation. There are personal triumphs and personal tragedies, but not a calling or a destiny in service of which greatness is exhibited. There is fate, but she is blind and, in her blindness, establishes a kind of equity among the warring parties. Both the nobility and the tragedy of heroes such as Achilles and Hector are set against a background of meaningless flux. Thus, Simone Weil writes that "[t]he progress of the war in the *Iliad* is simply a continual game of seesaw." What is absent is divine purpose—and, therefore, as Lewis notes, none of the events in the *Iliad* can have the kind of significance that the founding of Rome has in the *Aeneid*.

Aeneas's story is quite different. He is, Vergil tells us at the very outset, one who "came to Italy by destiny." Suffering countless setbacks both on land and sea—"so hard and huge / A task it was to found the Roman people"—still he was "[a] man apart, devoted to his mission." To be the man whom Heaven calls exacts a great price. Having already endured the ten-year siege of Troy and its fall, having lost his wife while making his escape with a small band of surviving Trojans, Aeneas must still suffer the wrath of Juno—storm, plague, and warfare—as he journeys from the ruins of Troy (on the western coast of modern Turkey) to Italy.

Seven summers after Troy's fall, Aeneas's company—still on the way—takes refuge from a storm at a port in Sicily. There they hold a festival to commemorate the death of Aeneas's father, Anchises. But in the midst of these games the Trojan women are moved to consider how long they have been wandering and how many hardships they have suffered.

> But on a desolate beach apart, the women
> Wept for Anchises lost as they gazed out
> In tears at the unfathomable sea.
> "How many waves remain for us to cross,
> How broad a sea, though we are weary, weary?"
>
> All had one thing to say: a town and home
> Were what they dreamed of, sick of toil at sea.

The women set fire to the ships, hoping—though unsuccessfully, of course—to compel the company to settle permanently in Sicily. They force Aeneas himself to wrestle with "momentous questions."

> Should he forget the destiny foretold
> And make his home in Sicily, or try
> Again for Italy?

Finally, he accepts the advice of Nautes that those "[t]oo weary of your great quest" should be permitted to remain behind and settle in Sicily. "Set them apart, and let them have their city / Here in this land, the tired ones."

A vocation exacts a price, and not all can pay it. Even though it may seem to draw us, its point is not happiness. It is, as C. S. Lewis notes, the nature of vocation to appear simultaneously both as desire *and* as duty. "To follow the vocation does not mean happiness; but once it has been heard, there is no happiness for those who do not follow." The price of a calling had been made clear to Aeneas himself even earlier. In one of the most famous books of the *Aeneid*, Vergil recounts the love affair of Aeneas and Dido. Their ships buffeted by a tremendous storm at sea, the Trojan company has made it to shore on the coast of North Africa, where the new colony of Carthage is being founded by a group of immigrants from Tyre and their queen, Dido.

Weary of the endless journeying to which Aeneas's destiny has committed them, the Trojans are glad to stay a while at Carthage while they repair their ships. Aeneas, in particular, finds happiness and seeming fulfillment in overseeing the work of building Carthage, and, ominously, he and Dido fall passionately in love. But when Jupiter learns this, he commands Mercury to remind Aeneas of the task he has been given.

> What has he in mind? What hope, to make him stay
> Amid a hostile race, and lose from view
> Ausonian progeny, Lavinian lands?
> The man should sail: that is the whole point.
> Let this be what you tell him, as from me.

"The man should sail." In the Latin, one word: *naviget!* The divine summons—which wounds even as it lures.

Mercury delivers the message, Aeneas hears and obeys. He gives orders to prepare the ships to sail, but, of course, Dido learns what is happening and begs him to stay.

> Duty Bound,
> Aeneas, though he struggled with desire
> To calm and comfort her in all her pain,
> To speak to her and turn her mind from grief,
> And though he sighed his heart out, shaken still
> With love of her, yet took the course heaven gave him
> And went back to the fleet.

Her sister Anna brings Dido's pleas to Aeneas, asking him at least to postpone his departure and not to leave so abruptly. "But no tears moved him . . . God's will blocked the man's once kindly ears." Aeneas has for the first time in a long time been happy and content in Carthage—sharing Dido's love, overseeing the work of construction. Dido seems finally to have found new love, years after the death of her husband, Sychaeus. The Trojan company seems to have found a place to settle.

But it is not the homeland to which they are called, and it is not the city Aeneas has been summoned to found. This is not his calling. "The man should sail." As Hook and Reno write, Vergil "does not wish us to cast our lot with Dido and our anachronistic ideas of authenticity." Do you want to know what is your vocation? Then the first question to ask is not, "What do I want to do with my life?" It is not as if I first come to know myself and then choose a vocation that fulfills and satisfies me. For it is only by hearing and answering the divine summons, by participating in my calling, that I can come to know who I am. We are not who *we* think we are; we are who *God* calls us to be. "The man should sail."

And sail he does—away from Carthage, willing to participate in his destiny. But perhaps for all readers, and certainly, I suspect, for at least some, a question presses insistently upon us. Hook and Reno sharpen the point when they write: "Aeneas sails away from Carthage changed, a greater hero in potential, but in most ways obvious to him and to us, a lesser man." That's the issue: Does obedience to his calling enhance or diminish Aeneas? That calling has drawn him away from ordinary human loves, it has compelled him to harden himself against quite natural emotions, it has brought upon him and those who accompany him countless hardships. That calling requires not that he seek to be himself, not that he ask first what he wants to do, not that he authentically determine his being—but that he obey. He says to Dido: "I sail for Italy not of my own free will" (*Italiam non sponte sequor*). One way to put all this is to note that for many readers of the epic Aeneas seems to become an almost divine figure, more than human, as his person is folded into his calling as founder of Rome. The other way to put it is to note that it can sometimes be hard to distinguish between one who is more than human and one who is, simply, inhuman. Especially for us, devoted as we are to authenticity and autonomy, the divine summons to obedience may seem to have left Aeneas diminished rather than enhanced. Such may be the price of a calling.

II

Is the price too great? Has Aeneas, in turning from authenticity to obedience, diminished his humanity? How we answer that question will tell us a good bit about ourselves. "I have read," C. S. Lewis writes,

> that his [Vergil's] Aeneas, so guided by dreams and omens, is hardly the shadow of a man beside Homer's Achilles. But a man, an adult, is precisely what he is: Achilles had been little more than a passionate boy. You may, of course, prefer the poetry of spontaneous passion to the poetry of passion at war with vocation, and finally reconciled. Every man to his taste. But we must not blame the second for not being the first. With Virgil European poetry grows up.

In an effort to understand, make sense of, and confirm Lewis's judgment we may recall another reader of Vergil.

In Book I of his *Confessions*, Augustine remembers how, as a boy, "I was forced to learn all about the wanderings of a man called Aeneas, while quite oblivious of my own wanderings." How sinful must he not have been, Augustine suggests, to care more about the wanderings of Aeneas in search of a homeland

than about the wanderings of his own soul away from the One
for whom he was made. "What indeed can be more pitiful than
a wretch with no pity for himself, weeping at the death of Dido,
which was caused by love for Aeneas, and not weeping at his
own death, caused by lack of love for you, God . . . ?" And yet,
at a deeper level, we must suppose that what Augustine learned
from Vergil may have reinforced what he was eventually to
learn from the scriptures, from his mother, Monica, and from
Ambrose.

The wanderings of Augustine's soul find their pattern in
the story of Aeneas. "I came to Carthage," Augustine writes at
the outset of Book III, conscious certainly that this was Dido's
Carthage, "and all around me in my ears were the sizzling and
frying of unholy loves." And years later, having decided to teach
rhetoric in Rome rather than Carthage, a decision opposed by
his mother, Augustine stole away on ship at night, going—like
Aeneas—from Carthage to Rome, and leaving a weeping woman
behind. This is the Augustine of whom, in that great scene in
the garden, Lady Continence asks what is essentially a vocational
question: "Why do you try and stand by yourself and so not
stand at all? Let him [God] support you." This is the Augustine
who, having been converted from the false ideal of personal authenticity and having handed over to God his broken will, torn
between desire and duty, concludes that he can be an authentic
self only in submission to God's call—concludes, indeed, that
only God can catch the heart and hold it still, that only God
can know him as he truly is. "There is still something of man,
which even the spirit of man that is in him does not know. But
you, Lord, know all of him, you who made him."

Thus, Augustine learned—more from the story of Jesus than
from that of Aeneas—"what the difference is between presumption and confession, between those who see their goal without
seeing how to get there and those who see the way which leads
to that happy country." That way was not anything Augustine
had done, his own hard and huge task; it was something that
had been done for him. What he found in the story of Jesus that
he had not found elsewhere was "the face and look of pity, the
tears of confession, your sacrifice." The story of Jesus's own

obedience makes clear that what looks like an annihilation of the
self may, in fact, be its enlargement. We flourish as we answer
obediently God's call. And this, in turn, has an important effect
on our understanding of vocation. As Hook and Reno observe,
the more we believe that God has himself done whatever needs
to be done and that our task is simply to answer his call, "the
less room appears to be left for our greatness, our achievement,
and accomplishment." Vocation, it seems, need no longer be
heroic—which brings us back to the other issue I identified at
the outset.

III

Consider, for example, the following passage from John Gals-
worthy's novel *One More River*, in which a character named
Dinny reflects on the death of old Betty Purdy.

> Death! At its quietest and least harrowing, but yet—death!
> The old, the universal anodyne; the common lot! In this bed
> where she had lain nightly for over fifty years under the low
> sagged ceiling, a great little old lady had passed. Of what was
> called "birth," of position, wealth and power, she had none. No
> plumbing had come her way, no learning and no fashion. She
> had borne children, nursed, fed and washed them, sewn, cooked
> and swept, eaten little, travelled not at all in her years, suffered
> much pain, never known the ease of superfluity; but her back had
> been straight, her ways straight, her eyes quiet and her manners
> gentle. If she were not the "great lady," who was?

Perhaps there is something heroic here, but nothing extraordinary. There is no quest for the great deed required by God.
There are only the everyday tasks, infused with the sense of
duty and dignity that may make it appropriate to describe them
as a calling.

When less room is left for our greatness and our achievement,
this is what ultimately happens to the idea of vocation. If the
seeds were already there in Augustine's rereading of the story
of Aeneas, it took centuries for this leveling or democratizing

of vocation to work itself out in the thought of the sixteenth-century Reformers. "The affirmation of ordinary life finds its origin," Charles Taylor writes, "in Judaeo-Christian spirituality, and the particular impetus it receives in the modern era comes first of all from the Reformation. . . . The highest can no longer be defined by an exalted *kind* of activity; it all turns on the *spirit* in which one lives whatever one lives, even the most mundane existence." That spirit is eloquently captured in George Herbert's poem "The Elixir," which reads in part:

> Teach me my God and King,
>   In all things thee to see,
> And what I do in anything,
>   To do it as for thee.
> . . . .
>   A servant with this clause
>   Makes drudgery divine;
> Who sweeps a room, as for thy laws,
>   Makes that and th' action fine.
>
>   This is the famous stone
>   That turneth all to gold:
> For that which God doth touch and own
>   Cannot for less be told.

This sentiment, both beautiful and powerful, intensifies our sense of vocation not by drawing us away from ordinary duties to some great quest but by drawing us more deeply into them. The strength—or, at least, one strength—of this shift is that the demands and the blessings of a calling are placed on every person. When a vocation is something as extraordinary and heroic as the huge labor of founding Rome—or, even, to take the example that more concerned the Reformers, something as extraordinary as the monastic life—it cannot be generally accessible. So, for example, in his well-known essay "Our Calling," Einar Billing, a Swedish Lutheran theologian of the early twentieth century, wrote: "The more fully a Catholic Christian develops his nature, the more he becomes a stranger to ordinary life, the more he departs from the men and women who move therein. But in the evangelical [he means Lutheran] church it cannot, it should and may not be. The evangelical church does not seek to create religious virtuosos, but holy and saintly men and women *in* the call." Now, Billing writes, "the demand to become a unique Christian character is put on each and every individual."

As those who have read Wingren on Luther, or Weber and Troeltsch on "innerworldly asceticism," will know, the power of such an understanding of vocation—sanctifying the work of every life, however humble—is undeniable, but it is by no means free of danger. The beauty of Herbert's poem notwithstanding, we should be hesitant to sanctify drudgery—as if one should not retire from it if one could. Still more, there is sometimes backbreaking and dangerous labor, or tedious and boring work, that must be done if we or our loved ones are to live, but the language of vocation imbues such work with a kind of meaning and significance that may seem unbelievable to those who must actually do it. They work to live; they do not live to work. Taken seriously, the sanctification of such laborious or tedious work with the language of vocation would suggest that we should struggle to find more time for it, not plot ways to escape it.

More important still, this sanctifying of ordinary work, this sense that it becomes exalted if only approached in the right spirit, may cause us to forget that a divine summons must not only hallow but also transform whatever we do. When the difference between a carpenter and a Christian carpenter, a historian and a Christian historian, a father and a Christian father, an artist and a Christian artist, a soldier and a Christian soldier—when all these differences are reduced to a matter of the "spirit" in which the work is done, we are well on our way to making the divine summons largely irrelevant. Whatever work we want to do—we'll just call that our vocation.

This is to nod at the call of God and go on our way; it is to lose the infinite, transforming horizon of God's call. To the degree that we collapse the divine call into the work we regularly do, work pretty much like that done by many others, we really collapse the two love commandments into one. We suppose that in loving the neighbor—and in no more than that—the love of God consists, as if we were made, ultimately, for work and not for rest in God.

IV

If we try to unify our lives through the idea of vocation—by supposing that God summons us only to good work pretty much like everyone else's work—we lose the infinite horizon of God's call. It was Augustine—again—who saw clearly that such a unified life cannot be ours in this world. When, at the beginning of Book XIX of his *City of God*, Augustine enumerates Varro's 288 possible answers to the question, "What is the good life?" and rejects them all, his rejection, as Peter Brown has written, "marks the end of classical thought." In place of the classical ideal of a unified life actually available to us here and now, Augustine substitutes the image of a pilgrim who must live in hope.

We should be equally clear that a life faithfully committed to the responsibilities of our vocation is not itself "the good life." God calls us not just to that but to himself—beyond every earthly joy or responsibility, beyond any settled worldliness which places its hope for meaning in those we love or the work we do. This lesson is taught unforgettably in Dante's *Divine Comedy*.

The engine that drives Dante's desire for the beatific vision is not simply love for God. It is love for that particular woman, Beatrice, whose beauty has drawn him every step of the way and through whose beauty he is being summoned beyond himself and toward the One who is Beauty itself. On his journey through hell and purgatory Dante has had Vergil as his guide. By the time we come to the end of the *Purgatorio*, in fact, Vergil has come to seem a permanent fixture on Dante's way. Then, in Canto XXX of the *Purgatorio*, Beatrice finally appears. And instantly, Dante writes,

> There came on me, needing no further sight,
>   Just by that strange, outflowing power of hers,
>   The old, old love in all its mastering might.

Overcome by emotion, Dante turns, as he has so often along
the way, to Vergil for reassurance—and Vergil is gone. He has
taken Dante as far as he may, as far as human wisdom is able,
but now love—love for that particular woman Beatrice as the
image of a still greater Beauty—must take Dante the rest of the
way. Tears come unbidden to his eyes, and Beatrice says:

> Dante, weep not for Virgil's going—keep
>   As yet from weeping, weep not yet, for soon
>   Another sword shall give thee cause to weep.
> . . . .
> Look on us well; we are indeed, we are
>   Beatrice. How hast thou deigned to climb the hill?
>   Didst thou not know that man is happy here?

The loss of Vergil, his master and guide, is a sword that pierces
Dante's soul—a necessary pain if he would see God. But an
even greater renunciation awaits Dante in Canto XXXI of the
Paradiso. In preparation for that renunciation we might recall
the scene in Book VI of the *Aeneid* when Aeneas, journeying
in the underworld to see his father, Anchises, confronts Dido
among the souls of those who have taken their own life. He
weeps as he speaks to her:

> I left your land against my will, my queen,
> The gods' commands drove me to do their will,
> . . . .
> And I could not believe that I would hurt you
> So terribly by going. Wait a little.
> Do not leave my sight.
> . . . .
>   But she had turned
> With gaze fixed on the ground as he spoke on,
> Her face no more affected than if she were
> Immobile granite or Marpesian stone.
> At length she flung away from him and fled,
> His enemy still, into the shadowy grove
> Where he whose bride she once had been, Sychaeus,
> Joined in her sorrows and returned her love.

Dido turns away from Aeneas—but not in hope for any new and greater love. Instead, she returns to an old love, and Aeneas takes up again his huge and hard task.

Not so for Dante as he journeys toward the vision of God. Beatrice has now taken him as far as she is able. She has brought him to the very brink of that final mystical vision shared by all the redeemed, she has prepared him to look upon the face of God. And, now, if he is to answer the divine summons, he must turn from image to reality. As Dante gazes at the snow-white rose that is filled with rank upon rank of the redeemed who look upon God, he turns to Beatrice that she may explain it to him.

And she is gone—returned to her place within those heavenly ranks. Looking up, Dante sees her "in her glory crowned, / Reflecting from herself the eternal rays," and he utters a plea that she continue to pray for him.

> Such was my prayer and she, so distant fled,
>   It seemed, did smile and look on me once more,
>   Then to the eternal fountain turned her head.

The austerity of that moment is overpowering. When we consider all that Dante has endured to find her, when we consider that it was she who had charged Vergil to be his guide, she who, as Dante says, "to bring my soul to Paradise, / Didst leave the imprint of thy steps in Hell," and when we consider that now—at last—he has come to her . . . seeing all that, we must see yet one thing more. It has, finally, been not the beauty of Beatrice but of God through Beatrice that has been summoning Dante all along the way. Having accomplished that, she turns her face away from him, once more to the eternal fountain. She does not leave him, nor he leave her behind, but together they are to gaze at the love that moves the sun and the other stars. It is not simply the beauty of Beatrice that has been summoning and drawing Dante, but God, and in looking away from him to God she does no harm to his joy or her own. "Didst thou not know that man is happy here?"

C. S. Lewis's *A Grief Observed*, written after the death of his
wife, Joy, ends with an evocation of this scene from the *Paradiso*.
Lewis writes: "She said not to me but to the chaplain, 'I am at
peace with God.' She smiled, but not at me." Likewise, in his
powerful and astringent chapter on charity in *The Four Loves*,
Lewis writes that "there is no good applying to Heaven for
earthly comfort. Heaven can give heavenly comfort; no other
kind. . . . We were made for God. Only by being in some respect
like Him, only by being a manifestation of His beauty, loving-
kindness, wisdom or goodness, has any earthly Beloved excited
our love. . . . It is not that we shall be asked to turn from them,
so dearly familiar, to a Stranger. When we see the face of God
we shall know that we have always known it."

Beyond and through every earthly love and every earthly
duty, we are to hear the call of God. On the one hand, we are
called to the God who can put an end to our work and bring
fulfillment to our loves and labors. "Didst thou not know that
man is happy here?" But on the other hand, this call will often
exact a price along the way—the price of renunciation, of huge
and hard labor. At times, to be sure, by God's grace, our calling
may bring considerable joy and satisfaction, but it cannot offer
settled contentment. For, as Augustine says, "It is one thing to
see from a mountaintop in the forests the land of peace in the
distance . . . and it is another thing to hold to the way that leads
there." Which is to say: For now, "the man should sail."

Notes

1. First published as "Divine Summons," *Christian Century*, 117 (November 1, 2000),
pp. 1110–18.

PART THREE

Freedom
for Embodied
Humanity

7

Between the Beasts and God[1]

Near the beginning of the twenty-fourth and last Book of Homer's *Iliad*, called by Simone Weil "the only true epic" the West possesses,[2] even the gods—detached as they are in their bliss from all suffering—have seen enough. Achilles has become inhuman. Ignoring our animal nature, our kinship with the beasts, he neither eats nor sleeps. Indeed, since the death of his friend and comrade Patroclus, the only food he wants is slaughter of the Trojans. "You talk of food?" he says to Agamemnon, who has argued that the Greek warriors must eat before they return to battle,

> I have no taste for food—what I really crave
> is slaughter and blood and the choking groans of men![3]

He has vowed, indeed, to throw twelve young Trojan warriors on the funeral pyre he will build for Patroclus—a human sacrifice to the memory of his friend. And, of course, he continues to tie the corpse of Hector to his chariot and drag it three times daily round dead Patroclus.

Achilles is inhuman. He cannot acknowledge the limits of bodily life—in particular, our mortality. He cannot acknowledge that we are less than immortal gods—and that, therefore, our actions must have limits and our lives must recognize bonds of human community across the generations. Another human being, a fellow human being, does not impose upon Achilles what Simone Weil called "that interval of hesitation" before one who is our equal in dignity.[4] Brilliant, proud, godlike Achilles . . . is not a man. Acknowledging no limits, acting as if he were himself more than human, he becomes in Homer's character-izations less than human—"like some lion, going his own bar-baric way" (24:48–49), "like inhuman fire raging on through the mountain gorges / splinter-dry" (20:54–55).

Apollo makes the case for stopping what is happening. "Achil-les has lost all pity! No shame in the man" (24:52). With the help of Zeus, Priam, the aged Trojan king, comes to Achilles' tent to plead for the return of the body of his son, Hector. In one of the most famous scenes in the history of our culture, Priam puts to his lips "the hands of the man who killed my son" (24:591) and reminds Achilles of the bond between the generations. "Remember your own father, great godlike Achil-les" (24:570).

> Those words stirred within Achilles a deep desire to grieve for his own father. Taking the old man's hand he gently moved him back. And overpowered by memory both men gave way to grief. Priam wept freely for man-killing Hector, throbbing, crouching before Achilles' feet as Achilles wept himself, now for his father, now for Patroclus once again, and their sobbing rose and fell throughout the house (24:592–99).

The gods may live free of such sorrows, Achilles tells Priam, but "we wretched men / live on to bear such torments" (24:613–14). The fact of human mortality undergirds the bond of human community. One generation dies that another may succeed it, though not without a sense of loss and sorrow. To be human is to be born of human parents, to have a place in the affective tie that binds together the generations of humankind.

"So come," Achilles says to Priam, "we too, old king, must think of food" (24:728). Acknowledging once again his own place within society and the limits of his mortal flesh, he eats, sleeps, and takes Briseis, now restored to him, to his bed. Commenting on the poem, Bernard Knox notes that now at last Achilles occupies "man's central position between beast and god."[5] He is no longer "godlike" Achilles, nor "some lion, going his own barbaric way." And precisely in being neither, his true humanity—in all its nobility, dignity, and pathos—is displayed.

Likewise, at the beginning of St. Mark's Gospel, Jesus, as the representative Israelite and therefore representative man, is depicted precisely as one who in his humanity stands between the beasts and God. Having been baptized by John and declared the beloved Son of God, Jesus is driven by the Spirit out into the wilderness to be tempted by Satan—the beginning of his great battle with Satan recorded in the Gospel. And, St. Mark writes, "he was with the wild beasts; and the angels ministered to him."[6] The beasts may be mentioned simply to accentuate the loneliness of the desert as a place of testing and struggle, but more probably "they are thought of as subject and friendly to" Jesus, and, hence, "the passage should be understood against the background of the common Jewish idea that the beasts are subject to the righteous man."[7] Cared for by the angelic servants of God, Jesus simultaneously exercises Adam's dominion over the animals. He stands where one who is truly human ought to stand—between the beasts and God. He occupies an "in-between."

The story of this true man culminates in a resurrection of the body—that is, in a vindication of the creation. It teaches us to honor the trajectory of human bodily life from birth to death—from the dependence that marks our birth to the dependence that marks our aging and dying. We are mortals, not immortals. But we are mortals whose special place in creation and whose longing for something more than this life alone can give have been vindicated by the triumph of Christ. We must learn to honor this bodily life without asking of it more than it can be or offer.

I

If this is what it means to be human, it may be no surprise that *bio*ethics—concerned as it is with *Bios*—should, especially at its most philosophical, focus so much attention on the beginning and end of life, on birth and death. For they are connected more profoundly than as simply the beginning and the end points of a life. To give birth to one like oneself, out of the very substance of one's being, is, even if only unwittingly, to nod in the direction of our mortality. Anyone who has had a child will recall how the experience of becoming a parent immediately gives one a different perspective on one's own parents. We stand in a line of succession. We give birth to those who take our place, even though they do not precisely re-place us.

If we stand between the beasts and God, we occupy a distinct place within the creation—a place that is passed on from parents to children in the act of begetting. One can deny this, of course, though not without paying a certain moral cost. Thus, for example, in his *Discourse on Inequality*, Rousseau allows himself to speculate about whether the "orang-outang" might be "a variety of man." We lack sufficient knowledge to decide, he says. "There would, however, be a method by which, if the 'orang-outang' and others were of the human species, the crudest observers could assure themselves of it even by demonstration; but since a single generation would not suffice for this experiment, it must be considered impracticable, because it would be necessary for what is only an hypothesis to be already proved true before the experiment that was to prove it true could be tried innocently."[8] Rousseau means, of course, that if human beings and "orang-outangs" could successfully interbreed, it would be demonstrated that they were of the same species. And we may suspect that Roussau's claim that the experiment could not be "tried innocently" unless it were known in advance that "orang-outangs" were themselves human may be less sincere than his playful willingness to contemplate—in the name, of course, of research—acts of bestiality that would deny any distinct place in the creation to humanity.

It should not really surprise us that Rousseau might toy with such possibilities. In his *Reveries of the Solitary Walker*, though doubting whether true happiness is attainable, he describes his notion of the kind of happiness appropriate to a human being as follows:

> But if there is a state in which the soul finds a solid enough base to rest itself on entirely and to gather its whole being into, without needing to recall the past or encroach upon the future; in which time is nothing for it; in which the present lasts forever without, however, making its duration noticed and without any trace of time's passage; without any other sentiment . . . except that of our existence, and having this sentiment alone fill it completely; as long as this state lasts, he who finds himself in it can call himself happy . . . with a sufficient, perfect, and full happiness which leaves the soul no emptiness it might feel a need to fill. . . .
>
> What do we enjoy in such a situation? Nothing external to ourselves, nothing if not ourselves and our own existence. As long as this state lasts, we are sufficient unto ourselves, like God.[9]

He wants to be godlike. Desiring that, he is bound to lose the sense of our humanity—that "in-between" place that distinguishes us not only from God but also from the beasts. Desiring to be like God, he can contemplate the possibility that he might be a fit mate for an "orang-outang."

In our own time, as we have come to think of ourselves more and more in terms of will and choice, Hobbes's "masterless men," we have transformed the meaning of birth. The bodily act of begetting, by which parents transmit their humanity to their children, can become an act of technical mastery over that part of nature which happens to be the human body. Here I do not bother to note the various ways in which we do this. Article after article tells the story. Nor will I give heed here to ways in which new reproductive technologies—or, should the day come, cloning—can subvert the meaning of parenthood. I will look from the other side—at what it means to be a child who is a product rather than a gift. Compare two rather different ways of picturing what it means to have a child.

We might—indeed, we have increasingly come to—picture it this way: Because having children is something people want for their life to be full and complete, because having children is an important project for so many people, we ought to use our technical skills to help them achieve what they desire—a child, and, quite possibly, a child of a certain sort. Indeed, having children—and, perhaps, children of a certain sort—is an entitlement to which there can be few limits. If the suffering and disappointment that infertility brings can be relieved, if people who desire a child can live more fulfilled lives by achieving that aim, then reproductive technologies are a good thing. We rightly use our technical mastery to augment human happiness by satisfying our individual projects, our desire for a child "of one's own." A story line of that sort increasingly dominates our thinking.

But compare that approach to a rather different image of the child. In Galway Kinnell's poem, "After Making Love We Hear Footsteps,"[10] the poet pictures the young child—awakened from sleep by the "mortal sounds" of his parents' lovemaking and propelled thereby "to the ground of his making," so that he "flops down" between his parents and "snuggles himself to sleep." They touch arms across his body and smile together at "this blessing love gives again into our arms." This child is by no means simply "his own," or "her own," or even (what is a little closer to the truth) "their own." We are pressed almost to eliminate that little word "own." This child is no one's product or project, but a gift received, a blessing given.

In the passion of sexual love a man and woman step out of themselves and give themselves to each other. Hence, we speak of sexual ecstasy—a word that means precisely standing outside oneself, outside one's own will and purpose. No matter how much they may desire a child as the fruit of their love, in the act of love itself they must set aside all such projects and desires. They are no longer making a baby of their own. They are giving themselves in love. And the child, if a child is conceived, is not then the product of their willed creation. The child is a gift and a mystery, springing from their embrace, a blessing love gives into their arms.

This makes a difference in how we understand the meaning of children. A product that we make to satisfy our own aims and projects is one whom we control—and, indeed, over whom we increasingly exercise "quality" control. A gift who springs from our embrace is one whom we can only welcome as our equal. We are not divine makers, but human begetters. And the child is not the product of our will, of any quasi-divine fiat, but, simply, one of us, who takes his or her place in the community of human generations.

II

Being of our being, these children are mortal. So ineluctably we find ourselves forced to think not only of birth but also of death. Here too the often admirable urge to do good all too easily becomes a desire for mastery without limits.

More than thirty years ago Paul Ramsey wrote chapter 3 of his *Patient as Person*.[11] That chapter, titled "On (Only) Caring for the Dying," remains one of the classic essays in bioethics. Thinking self-consciously from within a Christian perspective, Ramsey noted how our desire to master death can turn in two, seemingly quite opposite, directions. We may strive to extend life as long as possible, or may we decide to aim at death when the game no longer seems worth the candle. Seemingly opposite, these two tendencies within our culture both have their root in that same fundamental desire to be master of death. We will hold it at bay as long as we can, and we will embrace it when that seems to be the only way left to assert our mastery. Neither way acknowledges the peculiarly "in-between" place that human beings occupy in the creation.

"A living dog is better than a dead lion," says Koheleth, as if the nobility of human life were to lie only in its duration.[12] When our goal is simply to ward off death, to stay alive as long as possible, we miss an essential element in our humanity—the trajectory of bodily life that begins in dependence and moves, at the end, once again toward dependence and death. We miss our mortality. Perhaps more important still, we misdirect the longing buried at the heart of human existence.

Our hearts are restless, St. Augustine wrote, until they rest in God. That is, what the human heart desires is not simply more years. That offers quantity and continuance—which is more of the same—when what we desire is something qualitatively different. "Whatever has undergone no change certainly has *continuance*," Kierkegaard writes, "but it does not have *continuity*; insofar as it has continuance, it exists, but insofar as it has not won enduring continuity amid change, it cannot become contemporaneous with itself and is either happily unconscious of this misalignment or is disposed to sorrow. Only the eternal can be and become and remain contemporaneous with every age. . . ."[13] Even were we to master aging and dying, we would not have achieved the heart's desire; for the longing for God is not a longing for more of the same, more of this life. Were we simply another animal, our good might lie in warding off death and preserving bodily life. But we are not—and it does not. Standing between the beasts and God, our being opens us to God. The deepest chasm in our being is our need, not for more years, but for God.

Neither, however, should we embrace death—aim at it for ourselves or others—as if it were an unqualified good. "Whose life is it anyway?" I may ask. "Have I not been making decisions about this life of mine for years now? Should I not be free to end it if I wish?" Such questions come quite naturally to us, but to give them moral standing is to live a lie. We are earthly, mortal creatures whose being is, nonetheless, open to God. We are not just animals—for we are open to God. We are not gods—for we are open to God. Indeed, as the umbilical cord ought to remind us, we are never quite the independent individuals we like to think we are, and we deceive ourselves if we suppose that freedom is the sole truth of human existence. If we begin with the story of our creation, we have to say that the author of our being has authority over us. If we begin with the story of our reconciliation and say "Jesus is Lord," we have to say with St. Paul: "You are not your own; you were bought with a price. So glorify God in your body."[14] In either case, the project of mastering death—of aiming at it for ourselves or others—is a delusion, embracing as a good what should be, simply, undergone.

Here again, the temptation to be more than human may leave us less than human. Taking control of dying, taking aim at life—whether by euthanasia and assisted suicide or by simply withholding treatment so that the cognitively impaired will die—invites us to ignore our shared humanity. Not all born of human parents, not all who share in the bond of human generations over time, will seem equal in dignity—if and when those practices become accepted among us. To be equal in dignity it will then not suffice to be a member of the human community; it will be necessary to exercise the capacities of reason and will that make mastery possible. What seems at first like an expansion of our compassion—for those who lack these capacities—very quickly becomes a restriction of the scope of human community as they become candidates for elimination. From within the human community, the full number of those who occupy that "in-between" place, a great divide erupts. Some exercise godlike mastery, others (like the beasts) are put out of their misery.

III

To be human, then, is to learn to live and love within limits—the limits of our embodied, mortal life, the limits of those whose being opens to God. It is to acknowledge, honor, and esteem the particular place—between the beasts and God—that we occupy in the creation. One need not, however, contemplate for long the vision of humanity I have been developing before a certain problem inescapably arises. To accept—even to affirm and honor—such limits in our coming hither and our going hence is to accept suffering we might possibly relieve. It is to admit that there is good we might in our freedom accomplish which we should not attempt, because what we *do* counts for even more than what we *accomplish*. "The Fates have given mortals hearts that can endure," Apollo says, addressing the gods to argue that Achilles' inhumanity must be stopped (24:57). Achilles must somehow come to accept the meaning of mortal life, the limits that must be endured—not because we are unable to transcend them, but because we ought not. Can it be right to accept limits even on the good we might accomplish?

One response, of course, and it is a perfectly legitimate response, is to note that we may find other, morally acceptable ways to relieve suffering and do good. To the degree this is possible in any given instance, we have every reason to be glad and no reason to oppose it. But simply to take refuge in such hopes and possibilities is to make our life far too easy. We have to reckon with the fact that honoring the limits of our "in-between" condition may mean there is good which, in our freedom, we might accomplish but which we nevertheless decline to do. Can that possibly be reasonable?

Discussing some sermons of St. Augustine, first preached probably in the year 397 but newly discovered only in 1990, Peter Brown notes that Augustine was often required to preach at festivals of the martyrs. This was a time when the cult of the martyrs was of profound importance to the average Christian, for persecution was still a very recent memory. The martyrs were the great heroes, the "muscular athletes" and "triumphant stars" of the faith.[15] But, Brown suggests, one can see Augustine quite deliberately making the feasts of the martyrs "less dramatic, so as to stress the daily drama of God's workings in the heart of the average Christian."[16] For that average believer did not doubt that God's grace had been spectacularly displayed in the courage of the martyrs. What he was likely to doubt, however, was whether such heroism could possibly be displayed in his own less dramatic and more humdrum day-to-day existence. And so, Augustine points "away from the current popular ideology of the triumph of the martyrs to the smaller pains and triumphs of daily life."[17]

An example of how he does this is quite instructive for our purposes. "God has many martyrs in secret," Augustine tells his hearers. "Some times you shiver with fever: you are fighting. You are in bed: it is you who are the athlete."[18] Brown comments:

Exquisite pain accompanied much late-Roman medical treatment. Furthermore, everyone, Augustine included, believed that amulets provided by skilled magicians . . . did indeed protect the sufferer—but at the cost of relying on supernatural powers other than Christ alone. They worked. To neglect them was like neglecting any other form of medicine. But the Christian must not use them. Thus, for Augustine to liken a Christian sickbed to a scene of martyrdom was not a strained comparison.[19]

Here is a vision of life—and a rather noble one at that—for which "minimize suffering" is not the only or the primary imperative. It directs our attention not just to what we do or accomplish, but also to the kind of people we are.

A number of years ago, the philosopher J. B. Schneewind wrote an article with the seemingly puzzling title, "The Divine Corporation and the History of Ethics."[20] In it he sketched a way of understanding an ethic—the traditional, received Christian ethic—in which one's moral responsibilities are always limited. To be sure, Schneewind did this in part for the sake of explaining how modern moral philosophy had developed by turning away from that received ethic. But to understand it is to comprehend something of the vision of our humanity I have been unfolding.

Think of our world as a cooperative endeavor created, ordered, and governed by God. In it, as in any cooperative endeavor, participants play their roles, carry out the tasks assigned them, and in so doing join together to produce a good which none of them could have produced alone.[21] No one participant is responsible for achieving the good of the whole or the best overall good possible; yet the work of each is ordered toward that good. Sometimes individual agents will see more or less clearly how their tasks are related to the overall good, and in such cases they will need to take that into account and could perhaps be criticized if they simply ignored the general good while noting that they had fulfilled their assigned task. At such moments they need to act creatively in ways that are not simply given in any role.

There may be other times, however, when an individual cannot really see the larger good his assigned duty serves. In such cases, he cannot be criticized for ignoring the larger good while "minding his own business," for he simply doesn't know that larger good.[22] We can imagine a world in which the overall good is very important but also very complex, far too complex for any individual agent always to be sure of how his work contributes to achieving it. And we can also imagine that the supervisor in charge of this supremely important but very complex project is able to foresee problems and deal with emergencies, is fair in his supervision, and is good—"too good ever to assign any duties that would be improper from any point of view."[23] That world, imagined as a cooperative endeavor with God as that uniquely qualified supervisor, is the Divine Corporation.

Changing from a workplace metaphor to a more literary one, we might think of these agents as characters in a play. They know the part given them, and each must play it in his own way. But none of them is the dramatist or director, and none of them knows how the plot of the play is to be satisfactorily worked out. This is our situation. We are not the author but characters in the story—under authority. C. S. Lewis put the metaphor this way:

> We do not know the play. We do not even know whether we are in Act I or Act V. We do not know who are the major and who the minor characters. The Author knows. . . . That it has a meaning we may be sure, but we cannot see it. When it is over, we may be told. We are led to expect that the Author will have something to say to each of us on the part that each of us has played. The playing it well is what matters infinitely.[24]

Whichever metaphor we prefer, it is clear that if God recedes as a governing, directing, authorial presence whose responsibility it is to see to the good of the whole or work out the plot of the play, then human responsibility correspondingly increases and intensifies. That, as Schneewind suggests, is the story of modern moral philosophy.

Suppose a child is born with severe physical or mental de-
fects. Suppose someone suffers greatly while dying. Who bears
responsibility for that? Who must somehow make it good? In
something like that Divine Corporation model God is finally
responsible. Hence, we have centuries of reflection on theodicy.
But if God, that uniquely qualified supervisor, is eliminated
from the picture, either no one is to blame or we are. Either no
author is at work bringing the plot of this story to a satisfactory
conclusion, or we will have to sit down at the word processor
and assume that divine authorial responsibility. There is no
need for theodicy any longer, as if we needed assurance that
God would work things out. The need, rather, is that we should
see ourselves as responsible to make things work out. And so,
we are tempted to step out of our "in-between" place, to forget
that as we seek to be more than human we may become less
than human. We can see a practical illustration of this if we
consider the widespread—indeed, now almost routine—practice of prenatal screening of infants in the womb. If we are not
simply cooperators in and with a power greater than our own,
we are the life-givers, who bear responsibility for the quality of
the life we give. If we merely cooperate with a power greater
than our own, our task is to benefit as best we can the life this
child has. When we become the life-givers, we may be asked to
decide whether it is a benefit to have such a life.

Reaching that high, we may fall into a state less than human.
For in accepting such responsibility for the next generation, in
allowing ourselves even to suppose that it could be a fitting role
for human beings, we lose the fundamental human capacity to
love—to say to our children, to the next generation, "It's good
that you exist."[25] And once again, instead of equal human dignity
for all born of human parents, we will see a fundamental divide
erupt among us: Some will bear a quasi-divine responsibility.
Others, whose lives do not meet our standards, will be put out
of their misery. Better perhaps to learn to affirm and honor our
peculiar place between the beasts and God.

In accepting our limits, we accept the fact that there may be
suffering which could be relieved but ought not. Ought not
because there is no right way, no fittingly human way, to do so.

This does not mean, however, that those who suffer do so alone. Quite the contrary. Oliver O'Donovan, noting how suffering has become almost unintelligible for us, has helpfully distinguished between *compassion* and *sympathy*. "Sympathy is the readiness to suffer with others and enter into the dark world of their griefs. Compassion is the determination to oppose suffering; it functions at arm's length, basing itself on the rejection of suffering rather than the acceptance of it."[26] Since we cannot imagine suffering as our own willed project, and since we have come to suppose that all moral order has its ground in our will, suffering must, by definition, be morally unintelligible.[27] We can interpret it only as a defeat, though we may live to fight another day.

For Christians, the ills to which this mortal human life is subject, the sufferings we bear, are, as William F. May has put it, *"real,* but not *ultimate."*[28] They are real, sometimes terrible, and we must oppose them as best we can within the limits appropriate to creatures such as we are. But we cannot possibly take their measure rightly if, as May puts it, we "cannot believe that the decisive powers in the universe could possibly do anything worthwhile in and through the suffering" we and others undergo.[29]

However deep and profound our suffering, "the Fates have given mortals hearts that can endure." That is, though suffering and dying are a great crisis of this bodily life, the very deepest problem is the isolation and abandonment they seem to bring. Hence, if we are to endure, we need from others not just compassion but sympathy—that readiness to "enter into the dark world" of the sufferer. And if we are to make sense of our humanity, of the heavy yet limited responsibility we bear, the Divine Corporation will need more than just a uniquely qualified supervisor. That supervisor might be capable of compassion, but we will need sympathy.

IV

When, in that most famous of scenes, Priam comes to Achilles in his tent and they give way to their common grief, Achilles says:

Let us put our griefs to rest in our own hearts,
rake them up no more, raw as we are with mourning.
What good's to be won from tears that chill the spirit?
So the immortals spun our lives that we, we wretched
    men
live on to bear such torments—the gods live free of sor-
    rows (24:610–14).

But perhaps those are not the gods we need if we are to be fully human, for, living free of sorrows, they do not promise true sympathy. This is most strikingly apparent when Hector confronts Achilles, terrible in his power and anger, and Athena comes to Hector in the guise of his brother Deiphobus, promising to help him in the fight. "Come, let us stand our ground together—beat him back" (22:275).

"Deiphobus!"—Hector, his helmet flashing, called out
    to her—
"dearest of all my brothers, all these warring years,
of all the sons that Priam and Hecuba produced!
Now I'm determined to praise you all the more,
you who dared—seeing me in these straits—
to venture out from the walls, all for *my* sake,
while the others stay inside and cling to safety"
    (22:276–82).

Hector hurls his spear, but it glances off Achilles' shield.

He stood there, cast down . . .
he had no spear in reserve. So Hector shouted out
to Deiphobus bearing his white shield—with a ringing
    shout
he called for a heavy lance—
    but the man was nowhere near him,
vanished—
    yes and Hector knew the truth in his heart.
. . . .
I thought he was at my side, the hero Deiphobus—
he's safe inside the walls . . . (22:345–50, 352–53).

Rather different is the picture we find in Mark's Gospel. In that story, it is not too strong to say that *God* dies outside the walls of the city, sharing the mortality that marks human life. It is of the dead man on the cross that the centurion says, in the Gospel's climactic statement: "Truly this man was the Son of God!"[30] This God does not live free of sorrows. He accepts the mortality that marks our own "in-between" place—and is therefore also one of us. In a world governed by such a God, we can find and accept our place, we can live out the role given us in faith and hope. We can, that is, ourselves become fully human.

Notes

1. An earlier version of this essay appeared as "Between Beasts and God," *First Things*, no. 119 (January 2002), pp. 23–29.

2. Simone Weil, *The Iliad: or The Poem of Force* (Pendle Hill Pamphlet, no. 91, n.d.), p. 33.

3. Homer, *The Iliad*, translated by Robert Fagles, Introduction and Notes by Bernard Knox (New York: Penguin Books, 1990), 19:254–55. Other references to *The Iliad* will be given by book and line number (in the Fagles translation) in parentheses within the body of the text.

4. Weil, p. 14.

5. Bernard Knox, "Introduction," *The Iliad*, translated by Robert Fagles, p. 59.

6. Mark 1:13.

7. D. E. Nineham, *The Gospel of Mark* (Baltimore, MD: Penguin Books, 1969), p. 64.

8. Jean-Jacques Rousseau, *A Discourse on Inequality*, translated by Maurice Cranston (New York: Penguin Books, 1984), p. 158.

9. Jean-Jacques Rousseau, *The Reveries of the Solitary Walker*, translated by Charles E. Butterworth (New York: Harper & Row, 1982), pp. 68f.

10. Galway Kinnell, *Mortal Acts, Mortal Words* (Boston: Houghton Mifflin, 1980), p. 5.

11. New Haven and London: Yale University Press, 1970.

12. Ecclesiastes 9:4.

13. Søren Kierkegaard, *Works of Love*, translated by Howard and Edna Hong (New York: Harper Torchbooks, 1962), pp. 46f.

14. 1 Corinthians 6:19–20.

15. Peter Brown, *Augustine of Hippo* (Berkeley and Los Angeles: University of California Press, 2000), p. 454.

16. Ibid.

17. Ibid.

18. Ibid.

19. Ibid.

20. Richard Rorty, J. B. Schneewind, & Quentin Skinner (eds.), *Philosophy in History* (Cambridge University Press, 1984), pp. 173–91.

21. Ibid., p. 176.

22. Ibid., p. 177.

23. Ibid., p. 178.

24. C. S. Lewis, *The World's Last Night and Other Essays* (New York: Harcourt Brace Jovanovich, 1960), pp. 105f.

25. Josef Pieper, *About Love*, translated by Richard and Clara Winston (Chicago: Franciscan Herald Press, 1974), p. 19.

26. Oliver O'Donovan, *The Desire of the Nations* (Cambridge: Cambridge University Press, 1996), p. 276. The point is not a terminological one, and I am not certain our normal use of "compassion" and "sympathy" always corresponds to O'Donovan's distinction. Indeed, in *The Physician's Covenant* (Philadelphia: Westminster Press, 1983), William F. May uses the words in almost exactly an opposite sense: "By virtue of this deep identity with their children, parents also 'suffer with' them. Compassion marks the relationship. In this respect, parents also differ from philanthropists. A gulf separates the philanthropic giver from the receiver. The philanthropist may sympathize, but, qua philanthropist, he or she does not suffer with the beneficiary" (p. 39). Note that although O'Donovan and May use the terms in opposite ways, each makes a similar conceptual distinction—and the distinction is what counts.

27. Ibid., p. 277.

28. May, p. 70.

29. Ibid., p. 57.

30. Mark 15:39.

8

---ᗡ●ᑕ---

Genes as Resources[1]

I begin with some sentences from Ernest Hemingway's *The
Old Man and the Sea:*

He looked down into the water and watched the lines that
went straight down into the dark of the water. He kept them
straighter than anyone did, so that at each level in the darkness of
the stream there would be a bait waiting exactly where he wished
it to be for any fish that swam there. . . . I have no understanding of it and I am not sure that I believe in it. Perhaps it was a
sin to kill the fish. . . . He urinated outside the shack and then
went up the road to wake the boy. He was shivering with the
morning cold. . . . Then he was sorry for the great fish that had
nothing to eat and his determination to kill him never relaxed in
his sorrow for him. How many people will he feed, he thought.
But are they worthy to eat him? . . . That was the saddest thing
I ever saw with them, the old man thought. The boy was sad
too and we begged her pardon and butchered her promptly. . . .
The boy did not go down. He had been there before and one
of the fishermen was looking after the skiff for him.[2]

Hemingway's prose is, of course, generally regarded as clear and straightforward. And I suspect that any single sentence in the passage above was probably simple and transparent to you. I also suspect that, taken as a whole, the passage probably made almost no sense at all. There's a reason for that. The sentences in the passage are drawn from pages 29, 104–5, 22, 74, 48, and 123—*in that order.*

One of the great blessings of the computer age, our students are sometimes told, is that you can move sentences or whole paragraphs around with ease. You needn't really have a thesis and its accompanying arguments worked out when you sit down to write a paper. Just write—and then move the pieces around later. As if the argument of the paper were somehow built up from below—from words, phrases, and sentences moved around, combined and recombined. As if a thesis would just emerge without an organizing intelligence, an authorial perspective, at work from the outset. As if we could explain what is lower, the argument of the paper, without what is higher, the author.

My suggestion will be that we ought not make a similar mistake when we think about genes. Consider the image at work in the following frequently quoted passage from Thomas Eisner, a biologist from Cornell University:

> As a consequence of recent advances in genetic engineering, [a biological species] must be viewed as . . . a depository of genes that are potentially transferable. A species is not merely a hardbound volume of the library of nature. It is also a loose-leaf book, whose individual pages, the genes, might be available for selective transfer and modification of other species.[3]

Of Eisner's analogy, Mary Midgley comments: "The idea of improving books by splicing in bits of other books is not seductive because in books, as in organisms, ignoring the context usually produces nonsense."[4] I have tried to provide a humble illustration of this by splicing together sentences from different pages of just one book—producing thereby something unintelligible. And, letting our imaginations roam just a bit, I might also have spliced in sentences from *Anna Karenina* and *A Christmas Carol*—producing thereby an artifact we could not name. The problem with doing this is not only, as Midgley suggests, that we completely ignore context. It goes yet a little deeper. Such an image of a book ignores the presence of an authorial hand. It ignores the fact that a book is not just the sum of a number of words, sentences, or paragraphs. A book is a whole, with its own integrity.

I

This train of thought was first suggested to me by one of the findings of the Human Genome Project, a finding that got quite a bit of attention in news articles announcing (in February 2001) the completion of that project by two groups of researchers. We were told that the number of genes in the human genome had turned out to be surprisingly small. Thus, for example, we were informed that human beings have, at most, perhaps twice as many genes as the humble roundworm (downsized even more with new findings in 2004, so that human beings and roundworms have about the same number of genes), and that the degree of sequence divergence between human and chimpanzee genomes is quite small. Considering the complexity of human beings in relation to roundworms and, even, chimpanzees, it seemed surprising that, relatively speaking, much less complex organisms should not have far fewer genes than human beings.

Why, one might ask, should that seem surprising? It will be surprising if we assume that the complexity of a "higher" being is somehow built up and explained in terms of "lower" component parts (which serve as "resources"). If we explain the higher in terms of the lower, it makes a certain sense to suppose that a relatively complex being would need lots of component parts—at least by comparison with a less complex being. And, of course, one might argue that the Human Genome Project is "the ultimate product of an extreme reductionist vision of biology that has held that to understand better one need only to go smaller."[5]

Thinking about human beings that way is, in a sense, just the last stage in a long movement of Western thought. First we learned to think that qualities of objects were not really present in the object but were supplied by the knowing subject. Then some philosophers suggested that the objects themselves—and not just their qualities—were simply constructs of the knowing subject. But what happens when even that subject disappears? When this reductive process is applied to the human subject, we get, as C. S. Lewis noted in a witty passage,

> a result uncommonly like zero. While we were reducing the world to almost nothing we deceived ourselves with the fancy that all its lost qualities were being kept safe (if in a somewhat humbled condition) as "things in our mind." Apparently we had no mind of the sort required. The Subject is as empty as the Object. Almost nobody has been making linguistic mistakes about almost nothing. By and large, this is the only thing that has ever happened.[6]

In *The Abolition of Man* Lewis powerfully depicts the movement by which things came to be understood as simply parts of nature, objects that have no inherent purpose or telos—which objects can then become resources available for human use. Hence, the long, slow process of what we call conquering nature could more accurately be said to be reducing things to "mere nature" in that sense. "We do not," Lewis writes,

> look at trees either as Dryads or as beautiful objects while we cut them into beams: the first man who did so may have felt the price keenly, and the bleeding trees in Virgil and Spenser may be far-off echoes of that primeval sense of impiety. . . . Every conquest over Nature increases her domain. The stars do not become Nature till we weigh and measure them: the soul does not become Nature till we can psychoanalyze her. The wresting of powers *from* Nature is also the surrendering of things *to* Nature. As long as this process stops short of the final stage we may well hold that the gain outweighs the loss. But as soon as

we take the final step of reducing our own species to the level of mere Nature, the whole process is stultified, for this time the being who stood to gain and the being who has been sacrificed are one and the same.[7]

Although my central focus, like Lewis's, is on what happens to human beings when we think of them simply as collections of genes, it is important to note that this reductive understanding may be misplaced even when applied to lower creatures. Lewis himself suggests as much—that science does a kind of violence even to trees when understanding them simply as natural objects. In our own day, we have gone beyond the kind of quantitative reduction to parts that Lewis pictures. We are on the brink of losing organisms altogether. When organisms become things lacking entirely any self-definition, they become malleable and available for reprogramming. Biological boundaries between organisms become "historically contingent products of gradually accumulated genetic change," and, therefore, those boundaries can be "slightly breached with only slight consequences."[8] Living beings, including human beings, become collections of bits of genetic information to be combined and recombined in countless possible ways. At one time we might have thought that the scientific attempt to understand the higher in terms of the lower was just that: a search to understand. Now, however, wisdom gives way to power. For now there may be nothing there to know—except what we assemble and create. And genes are the resource we use in this creative process.

Within the discipline of bioethics this approach will have its effect via a theory of justice. Begin in this genetic age to think of human beings as constituted by their parts, and you will find yourself thinking of genes as resources which may or may not be justly distributed. Even as we might think about the just distribution of wealth, or food, or education, or medical care, so also we might think of the bundles of genes that—on this view—constitute our selves as simply another resource, which can be distributed justly or unjustly.

For an older way of thinking there were human beings and there were resources. We did justice or injustice *to* human beings by what we did *with* those resources. But now we will be invited to think of justice or injustice in the *making* of human beings—which is what we do when we distribute genetic resources.[9] And, in fact, going one step further, there will be no compelling reason to think that the genetic resources to be distributed need be confined to DNA from the human species.[10] Human beings are simply creatures to be fashioned out of available genetic resources, and the only moral question will be whether those resources are fairly distributed.

II

But somewhere back in the depths of that consciousness which we will still imagine ourselves to have, we may detect a nagging worry. Who exactly are these beings who make decisions about how to distribute our genetic resources? What entitles them to make such judgments? In a world devoid of any inherent value or purpose, in which organisms lack any self-definition, it's not clear that we should be talking about justice or injustice. Why should we think some people wronged if they do not get a fair share of genetic endowments? That may be their misfortune, but what responsible agent has wronged them? In such a world, we cannot blame God or, even, Nature with a capital "N."

Justice or injustice can be nothing more than a construct we impose—not only upon ourselves, but also upon those future generations whom we fashion from the genetic resources we distribute. We have, in fact, no moral ground for anointing one particular distribution as more just than another. What we have is creative power. This is what happens when we can no longer blame something higher—God or Nature—for our condition.

Unless, of course, we are god—or, at least, some of us are. Let us suppose that neither God nor Nature can any longer be held responsible for the future of the human condition. But suppose also that we remain morally serious. We believe it makes a difference, a moral difference, how genetic resources are distributed to future generations. If neither God nor Nature is available to shoulder that moral burden, but if seriousness requires that someone shoulder it, who remains as a likely candidate for such responsibility? Only, I think, humanity—now conceived as godlike in its utterly free creative power and its responsibility for the future.

The vision that underlies the view of genes as resources is powerful and appealing precisely because of this mythic dimension. Rather than thinking of organisms as the result of an evolutionary process (generated by natural selection), we may think of organisms as self-creators, constantly organizing and reorganizing themselves by reordering their genes. Thus, genetic engineering, as a continual exercise of our freedom, is in accord with nature; it is nature's way of generating the ongoing evolutionary process. If we miss the powerful mythic, religious dimensions of this account—if we think of it simply as a neutral, scientific picture of the universe—we will miss much of its appeal. For example, Lee Silver ends his book *Remaking Eden* imagining some future generation of "GenRich" creatures, for whom *homo sapiens* had been a distant ancestor.

> These beings have dedicated their long lives to answering three deceptively simple questions that have been asked in every self-conscious generation of the past.
> "Where did the universe come from?"
> "Why is there something rather than nothing?"
> "What is the meaning of conscious existence?"
> Now, as the answers are upon them, they find themselves coming face to face with their creator. What do they see? Is it something that twentieth-century humans can't possibly fathom in their wildest imaginations? Or is it simply their *own* image in the mirror, as they reflect themselves back to the beginning of time . . . ?[11]

This is not science, of course; it is myth. It could not possibly appeal to us as powerfully as it does were it not for that mythic dimension, and as such it invites our sustained attention and critique. That is to say, we should take its mythic character seriously and think about the kind of moral commitments it involves when we do so.

This myth is, first and most important, radically dualistic.[12] When genes become resources and organisms lack self-definition, they become amenable to indefinite reprogramming. For a long time human beings contented themselves with the pleasant thought that they were subjects who objectified and constructed the rest of the world. Now, however, we too become constructs, as our genes are spliced and exchanged. But, then, who is doing the programming? Whose project are we? Clearly, there is a ghost in the machine, as dualists have always believed. We are both programmer and programmed, both manufactured body and ethereal manufacturer. And where do these two come together, if not in the pineal gland? We cannot say. But it appears that the real self can hardly be a body; for the body can be shaped and reshaped as we distribute genetic resources.

The initial dualism, therefore, is metaphysical. In what looks at first to be a materialist, reductionist age, bodily form is indefinitely malleable. But the real self—that powerful, creative, ordering intelligence—is not body. It must be something different. For any future our impoverished imaginations can conceive, that real self no doubt needs the body as a kind of beachhead in our world—a mode of entry by means we cannot fathom. But the body is, finally, mere natural object. For the real self—the creative, constructive self—we will have to look elsewhere.

Were this the end of the dualism, were it merely an idea, perhaps it would do little harm. But ideas have a way of taking shape in life, and if sheer metaphysical dualism of body and self cannot really be lived, those who think in its terms will find a vulgar translation. In place of the dualism that separates the ghost in the machine from the body will come the dualism that separates some human beings (the programmers) from others (the programmed). Who will undertake to design our future descendants? "It cannot be the human race as a whole," Mary Midgley writes,

> they wouldn't know how to do it. It has to be the elite, the biotechnologists who are the only people able to make these changes. So it emerges that members of the public who complain that biotechnological projects involve *playing God* have in fact understood this claim correctly. That phrase, which defenders

of the projects have repeatedly dismissed as mere mumbo jumbo, is actually a quite exact term for the sort of claim to omniscience and omnipotence on these matters that is being put forward.[13]

In short, the very first moral casualty of this dualism is human equality in the relation between the generations; for Midgley is, in effect, echoing the point made by C. S. Lewis a half century earlier: "Each new power won *by* man is a power *over* man as well."[14]

There is a second thing to notice about this myth, namely, how powerfully religious it is. Perhaps it is good to remember that when the magician Merlin makes his appearance in Geoffrey of Monmouth's twelfth-century *History of the Kings of England*, he is both magician *and* engineer. In the kingdom of Britain there is no one more skilled "either in the foretelling of the future or in mechanical contrivances."[15] It is Merlin who oversees and enables the engineering marvel of moving to Britain the rocks that form Stonehenge; it is also he who magically disguises King Utherpendragon so that, seeming to be Gorlois, Duke of Cornwall, he may sleep with the duke's wife, Ygerna, by whom Arthur is conceived. That powerful capacity to engineer and reconstruct is intimately related to the magician's desire to tap into power more-than-human, and for precisely that reason genuine science must be governed by a sense of limits.

We should not underestimate how deeply this desire for a godlike power infects our humanity. It is, after all, central to such stories as the Fall of Adam and Eve, or that of Prometheus. Because this desire—which is ultimately a desire not for wisdom but for power—infects us so deeply, we do well to anticipate that even the most altruistic of our projects may be corrupted by it. When a religious quest goes bad, after all, it becomes demonic. The sense that we can treat our genes as resources to be combined and recombined indefinitely has been called "algeny," a name intended to remind us of "alchemy," the quest to transform base metals into gold, which was itself both scientific and religious in character. If we do not see these connections, we miss the human meaning of what is happening in genetic advance, and we fail to see how the thirst that drives and underlies the bioengineering project may sometimes be idolatrous.

Dualistic and religious in character, this great mythic vision of genes as resources, this sense that we might have within our grasp a power very near the secret of life, is also utopian. The project of human improvement, of overcoming suffering and enhancing capacities, knows no end. There will always be another disease to overcome, more years to be added to life, more points to be added to the intelligence quotient. Jeremy Rifkin, who was largely responsible for popularizing the term "algeny," has noted how the alchemical quest "was to help nature in its struggle to 'perfect itself.'"[16] Likewise, Rifkin suggests, the "algenist is the ultimate engineer."[17] Cooperating with a nature understood to have only very fluid boundaries between organisms, treating genes as resources to be combined in ever new and better ways, we place our hope—and, in a sense, our virtue—in the future. If that perfected future never comes, or if it comes and turns out to be one marked by power rather than wisdom, we will have to be justified by only our good intentions, and I doubt that they are adequate for the task.

III

If this does not sound like a desirable path into the future, perhaps we need to rethink the image of genes as pages in a loose-leaf book, to be transferred and combined at will. We need, that is, to rethink the meaning of our humanity. Can we at least begin to contemplate other, more satisfactorily human, ways of thinking about our humanity?

Anything I say here must be inadequate, but it is important that we begin this process of rethinking. Rather than understanding the human being—the higher organism—in terms of what is lower, we may need to recapture a way of thinking that begins with what is higher and does not think of human beings as collections of bits of genetic information. "[T]he key to complexity," Stephen Jay Gould wrote shortly after the findings of the genome project were announced, "is not more genes, but more combinations and interactions generated by fewer units of code—and many of these interactions (as emergent properties, to use the technical jargon) must be explained at the level of their appearance, for they cannot be predicted from the separate underlying parts alone. So organisms must be explained as organisms, and not as a summation of genes."[18]

If we insist on starting from below in thinking about our human nature, we will miss much of the depth of the human person.[19] Imagine someone who wants to translate from a language with a large, varied, and subtle vocabulary into a language with a much smaller and less varied vocabulary. How can one do this? Only by giving more than one sense to words in the language into which we are translating. And, of course, a speaker of that language—who knew only it—might obstinately insist, "No, that's not the right way to use this word." He would be approaching the richer language from below, as if the richer could be made up simply of words drawn from the limits of his own, less subtle language, and he could never acquire insights and wisdom available only in that richer language.

Likewise, a man in love with a woman and a man lusting after a woman may experience many of the same physiological "symptoms." If we have never been in love, or if we insist on acting as if we have never been in love—if, that is, we persist in looking at the experience only from below, in terms of its physiological symptoms—we might argue that there is no difference between love and lust. The theory a man would be too wise to enunciate when he whispered in her ear might seem a compelling thesis for a scholarly essay. Only one who began from above, who knew what it was to be in love, would see at once that these experiences are not the same. If, however, we insist that love must be analyzed and understood entirely in terms of those physiological symptoms, we cut ourselves off from an entire realm of human wisdom. We will never know what it means to be in love.

Were we really to think of human beings from above, to eschew, at least for certain moments and purposes, reductionistic modes of thought, it would be no surprise for us to learn that the relative "richness" of human life is not simply a matter of our having more genes than other organisms. Thinking from above, we would stop thinking about human beings simply as collections of resources, which it was our duty to distribute in creatively fashioning the next generation. We would be protected, at least somewhat, against thinking of our relation to future generations chiefly as an exercise of power in the making and remaking of humanity—even if such power is cloaked in the language of a theory of justice. In short, were we to master the genies who invite us to think and desire in certain ways, we would have far less to fear from the ongoing attempt to master our genes.

Notes

1. An earlier version of this essay was published under the same title in *The Hedgehog Review*, 4 (Fall 2002), pp. 66–79.

2. Ernest Hemingway, *The Old Man and the Sea* (New York: Charles Scribner's Sons, 1952), pp. 29, 104–5, 22, 74, 48, 123.

3. "Chemical Ecology and Genetic Engineering: The Prospects for Plant Protection and the Need for Plant Habitat Conservation," Symposium on Tropical Biology and Agriculture, St. Louis, MO, Monsanto Company (July 15, 1985). Cited in Mary Midgley, "Biotechnology and Monstrosity," *Hastings Center Report*, 30 (September–October 2000), p. 11.

4. Midgley, p. 12.

5. Alfred I. Tauber and Sahotra Sarkar, "The Human Genome Project: Has Blind Reductionism Gone Too Far?" *Perspectives in Biology and Medicine*, 35 (Winter 1992), p. 228. I have eliminated italics from this citation.

6. C. S. Lewis, "Preface" to *The Hierarchy of Heaven and Earth*, by D. E. Harding (London: Faber and Faber, 1952), p. 10.

7. C. S. Lewis, *The Abolition of Man* (New York: Macmillan, 1947), pp. 82–83.

8. Stuart A. Newman, "Carnal Boundaries: The Commingling of Flesh in Theory and Practice," in Lynda Birke and Ruth Hubbard (eds.), *Reinventing Biology* (Bloomington and Indianapolis: Indiana University Press, 1995), p. 222.

9. Allen Buchanan, Dan W. Brock, Norman Daniels, and Daniel Wikler, *From Chance to Choice: Genetics and Justice* (Cambridge University Press, 2000), p. 85.

10. Ibid., p. 87.

11. Lee M. Silver, *Remaking Eden: Cloning and Beyond in a Brave New World* (New York: Avon Books, 1997), p. 250.

12. Cf. Newman, pp. 221–22; Midgley, p. 12.

13. Midgley, p. 14.

14. Lewis, *Abolition of Man*, p. 71.

15. Geoffrey of Monmouth, *The History of the Kings of Britain*, translated by Lewis Thorpe (New York: Penguin Books, 1996), p. 195.

16. Jeremy Rifkin, *The Biotech Century* (New York: Jeremy P. Tarcher/Putnam, 1998), p. 34.

17. Ibid., p. 35.

18. Stephen Jay Gould, "Humbled by the Genome's Mysteries," *New York Times*, February 19, 2001, p. A21.

19. The examples in this and the next paragraph are drawn from C. S. Lewis, "Transposition," in *The Weight of Glory* (Grand Rapids: Eerdmans, 1949). See especially pp. 19–21.

9

The Point of a Ban: Or, How to Think about Stem Cell Research[1]

In its report titled *Ethical Issues in Human Stem Cell Research*, the National Bioethics Advisory Commission (NBAC) said the following of the congressional ban on federally funded embryo research: "In our view, the ban conflicts with several of the ethical goals of medicine, especially healing, prevention, and research. . . ."[2] So inured have we become to such language that we fail to notice its oddity. Is it surprising that a ban should conflict with desirable goals? Or isn't that, in fact, why we sometimes need a ban—precisely to prohibit an unacceptable means to otherwise desirable ends? Taking note of this point—the oddity of the sentence I cited—should help us think about the issue of stem cell research.

To explore the logic of and make sense of a ban on stem cell research is my aim here. To be sure, such a ban may have persuasive appeal chiefly for those who are concerned to affirm the dignity of the embryo, but our public debate has for the most part been restricted to a seemingly endless argument about its status. Given the fact that many parties to the debate claim, at least, to agree that the embryo should be treated with "respect," perhaps it may be fruitful to explore other issues—in particular, issues involving the nature of moral reasoning and the background beliefs that underlie such reasoning. I propose, therefore, to take a very long way round. Our understanding of what is at stake can be sharpened if we begin not with stem cell research but with a quite different moral question.

In the memoir of his service as a Marine in the Pacific theater of World War II, historian William Manchester writes at one point:

> Biak was a key battle, because Kuzumi had made the most murderous discovery of the war. Until then the Japs had defended each island at the beach. When the beach was lost, the island was lost; surviving Nips formed for a banzai charge, dying for the emperor at the muzzles of our guns while few, if any, Americans were lost. After Biak the enemy withdrew to deep caverns. Rooting them out became a bloody business which reached its ultimate horrors in the last months of the war. You think of the lives which would have been lost in an invasion of Japan's home islands—a staggering number of American lives but millions more of Japanese—and you thank God for the atomic bomb.[3]

Yet one might argue—many have—that it would always be wrong to drop atomic bombs on cities, that doing so violates the rights of non-combatants. One might argue for a ban on that approach to waging war, even though in the instance cited by Manchester one can reasonably claim that such a ban would have conflicted with several of the ethical goals of statecraft: to minimize loss of life, and to seek peace and pursue it.

I

How do we reason about such a ban in the ethics of warfare? There are, of course, different views about what is permitted in war, as there are different views on all important moral questions. But if we contemplate briefly the logic of one very widely read treatment—Michael Walzer's *Just and Unjust Wars*[4]—we will discover that it provides a helpful window into our consideration of banning federal support for stem cell research.

Walzer notes—following a well-trodden path—that there is a kind of dualism in just war theory. It requires two different sorts of moral judgments—about when it is permissible to go to war (what Walzer calls "the theory of aggression") and what it is permissible to do in war (which he terms "the war convention"). These are two different sorts of judgments. If we are fortunate, they will cohere for us: that is, those who have just cause for going to war will be able to win without fighting in ways that are prohibited. Because, however, these really are two different moral judgments, there are moments when we face "dilemmas of war," when it may seem, for example, that those whose cause is just cannot win unless they violate the war convention.

Confronted by such a dilemma, we might reason in several different ways. We might adopt a simple utilitarian approach, and, as Walzer notes, "[i]t is not hard to understand why anyone convinced of the moral urgency of victory would be impatient" with the notion of a ban on certain means to that victory (p. 227). The more desirable the goals we pursue, the more tempting it will be to allow seemingly obvious utilitarian calculations to carry the day. If we take this route, the war convention provides us with, at best, rules of thumb—some general guidelines about how to fight, which, however, may be set aside whenever they conflict with the means required for those with just cause to win. To reason thus is, in effect, to conclude that the morality of war really involves only one kind of moral judgment: about when it is permissible to go to war. There is no genuine "dualism" in just war theory.

In an effort to preserve at least some sense that two different sorts of moral judgments are present, we might turn to what Walzer calls a "sliding scale." Roughly speaking, it means: although there may be some rules that should never be violated, "the greater the injustice likely to result from my defeat, the more rules I can violate in order to avoid defeat" (p. 229). Hence, the sliding scale is simply a gradualist way of eroding the distinction between just war theory's two kinds of moral judgments. "The only kind of justice that matters is *jus ad bellum*" (p. 230). The sliding scale is simply the timid person's avenue to utilitarian calculation.

The true alternative to such calculation seems to be a kind of moral absolutism: do justice even if the heavens fall. "To resist the slide, one must hold that the rules of war are a series of categorical and unqualified prohibitions, and that they can never rightly be violated even in order to defeat aggression" (p. 230). This does, at least, acknowledge the force of each sort of moral judgment we make about war—what goals it would be desirable to realize, and what rights it is necessary to respect—and it permits the tension between these judgments to stand. It does not deny that winning in a just cause is often very important indeed; it simply refuses to reduce reasoning about how to fight to calculations of how best to win, and it does not gradually chip away at the rights recognized by the war convention by means of any sliding scale. In short, it acknowledges that a ban on fighting in certain ways will certainly make it more difficult to achieve the good ends sought in war, but it does not offer that fact as, in itself, an argument against such a ban. The morality of warfare involves both judgments about values to be realized and rights to be upheld. When important values cannot be realized without violating rights, it would be peculiar simply to note this fact as an argument in favor of violating rights—as if a ban on such violation were out of the question. It might be that we should do justice even if the heavens will fall, even if those values cannot then be realized or must be pursued in some slower, less certain, manner.

For such a position Walzer has considerable respect. Nevertheless, he himself adopts "an alternative doctrine that stops just short of absolutism. . . . It might be summed up in the maxim: do justice unless the heavens are (really) about to fall" (p. 231). This "utilitarianism of extremity" does not commit us to reasoning in terms of a sliding scale. Whether one's cause is relatively more or less just, the rules of the war convention apply with equal force, and we are not to chip away gradually at its limits. Ordinarily, in fact, a nation with just cause ought to accept defeat rather than try to win by fighting unjustly. Sometimes, however, in very special circumstances, a nation at war may face an enemy who simply "must" be defeated, whose possible victory constitutes "an ultimate threat to everything decent in our lives" (p. 253). The paradigmatic example of such an enemy, for Walzer, is the Nazi regime.

Confronting such an enemy, facing a defeat that threatens everything decent in human life, there might come a moment when we simply had to override the war convention and fight unjustly. This is no gradual erosion of moral limits such as the sliding scale permits. It is, rather, "a sudden breach of the convention, but only after holding out for a long time against the process of erosion" (p. 231). The limits remain in place—until the moment when we must reason in accord with a utilitarianism of extremity and override them.

How shall we recognize such a moment of supreme emergency—and, just as important, how not suppose that we face such a moment every time we are tempted to fight unjustly in a good cause? Walzer offers two criteria to help us delimit the moment, though, of course, criteria alone can never replace the discernment of wise men and women. It must be both strategically and morally necessary to override the war convention. No other strategy must be available to oppose the enemy, and the enemy must really constitute an ultimate threat to moral values. The moment is upon us only when we face an enemy who can be beaten in no other way (strategic necessity) and who must be beaten (moral necessity). For Walzer, Britain's decision to bomb German cities—a decision made late in 1940—responded to such a moment of supreme emergency.[5] Civilians were targeted and the war convention overridden. Necessary though this may have been, Walzer argues that even in a moment of supreme emergency the war convention is "overridden," not "set aside." Despite the logical difficulties facing that assertion, he argues that political leaders who undertake such deeds bear a burden of criminality—though they do what they must according to a utilitarianism of extremity.

The passage from William Manchester with which I first directed our attention to the ethics of warfare might be thought to make such an argument from supreme emergency. "You think of the lives which would have been lost in an invasion of Japan's home islands . . . and you thank God for the atomic bomb." Walzer, however, believes the decision to drop the atomic bomb on Hiroshima was unjustified, and he argues that the American government did not, then, face a moment of supreme emergency which necessitated a breach of the war convention. American policy sought from Japan an unconditional surrender, and Japanese policy was to make an invasion so costly that the Americans would prefer to negotiate a settlement. "[T]he continuation of the struggle was not something forced upon us. It had to do with our war aims. The military estimate of casualties was based not only on the belief that the Japanese would fight almost to the last man, but also on the assumption that the Americans would accept nothing less than unconditional surrender" (p. 267).

Since, however, the Japanese government was not—in Walzer's view—the moral equivalent of the Nazi regime, there was no imperative reason to demand unconditional surrender. It "should never have been asked" (p. 267). Of course, it would have been morally desirable—very desirable—to end the war quickly. And yes, it would have been morally desirable to end the war with a clear-cut victory. And of course it was morally desirable to minimize the loss of life. One can imagine those whose lives would have been lost had we refused to drop the bomb arguing that we might have saved them had we been less scrupulous. All that, however, provided—in Walzer's judgment—no persuasive reason to override the war convention. Hence, the ban on bombing cities should never have been set aside here—good though the cause undeniably was. To say "the ban on bombing civilians conflicts with several of the ethical goals of warfare and must therefore be set aside" would have been morally mistaken.

Two other features of Walzer's analysis need notice here before we turn to the issue of stem cell research. The first concerns his discussion of "The Dishonoring of Arthur Harris," and the second attends to the problem of nuclear deterrence. The very concept of supreme emergency presumes that, almost always, the limits marked off by inviolable rights remain in place. Those limits are transgressed only in the most extreme instance of moral and strategic necessity. And they are never simply "set aside"; they are "overridden." Having been overridden, they must then be put back into place. Those who transgressed the ban and fought unjustly bear a burden of criminality. Walzer does not suppose that nation-states, especially victorious ones, could—or should—legally punish responsible leaders, but he does think that, after the fact, a way must be found to reinstate the overridden moral code. Thus, Arthur Harris, chief of Britain's Bomber Command, who advocated bombing civilians and whose pilots carried out that terrorist policy, was the only one of Britain's top wartime commanders not rewarded after the war with a seat in the House of Lords. This "refusal to honor Harris," Walzer writes, "at least went some small distance toward re-establishing a commitment to the rules of war and the rights they protect." Supreme emergency must be a "moment." It must come to an end, and the moral law must be reacknowledged and reinstated.

To see that is to understand why one of the least successful features of Walzer's analysis of just war theory is his discussion of nuclear deterrence. The moral problem of deterrence—especially acute during the Cold War but still troubling today—is that one targets civilians, threatening almost unimaginable destruction, in order to avoid war altogether. For the many years of nuclear standoff between the U.S. and the Soviet Union, this deterrence posture seemed to work (at least in the sense that nuclear weapons were used only to deter and not to fight). Walzer tries to make sense of this by suggesting that "[s]upreme emergency has become a permanent condition. Deterrence is a way of coping with that condition, and though it is a bad way, there may well be no other that is practical in a world of sovereign and suspicious states. We threaten evil in order not to do it, and the doing of it would be so terrible that the threat seems in comparison to be morally defensible" (p. 274). The benefits are so great, in fact, that, horrifying as it is in principle, deterrence can become, Walzer notes, "easy to live with" (p. 271). The needed reinstatement of the moral code is deferred—indefinitely. It is hard to find this persuasive. Having resisted any too easy transgressing of rights and limits, having confined utilitarian calculation to the moment of supreme emergency, Walzer simply settles for a permanent condition of supreme emergency. But, of course, when all moments are catastrophic, none is. In the dark of night all cats become gray, and we lose the ability to make needed and important moral distinctions.

II

In an article that draws on an analogy between war and research, Glenn McGee and Arthur Caplan argue for the moral justifiability—perhaps, even, obligatoriness—of stem cell research.[6] They suggest that NBAC and other scholars have been too ready to accommodate research opponents who would ban any research that involves deliberate destruction of embryos. Ceding too much ground to these opponents, advocates of research, although they argue for moving ahead (if with caution), never directly confront the objection. By contrast, McGee and Caplan argue that, even if one grants the humanity and personhood of the embryo, its destruction in stem cell research is justified because this research promises to relieve incalculable suffering. Therefore, "the moral imperative of compassion . . . compels stem cell research" (p. 153). The "central moral issues in stem cell research" have to do, McGee and Caplan say, "with the criteria for moral sacrifices of human life" (p. 152). (It is instructive to note that they tend to talk not about when life may be "taken," but when it may be "sacrificed" or "allowed to die." Clearer language would make for a clearer argument.) Even if one grants the personhood of the embryo, they argue that, at least for most of us, this cannot determine whether its life may be taken. Only those who oppose all killing of any kind "can rationally oppose the destruction of an embryo solely by virtue of its status as a human person" (p. 153). So, for most of us who do not oppose all killing as unjustified, the question becomes: "What constitutes unwarranted violence against an embryo, and for what reasons might an embryo ethically be destroyed—e.g., in the interest of saving the community?" (p. 153).

When, if ever, is it permissible to sacrifice a human life in service of the common good? When is such killing warranted? For McGee and Caplan, at least, "it is clear that . . . no need is more obvious or compelling than the suffering of half the world at the hand of miserable disease. Not even the most insidious dictator could dream up a chemical war campaign as horrific as the devastation wrought by Parkinson's disease . . ." (pp. 155f.). Since it would be possible, McGee and Caplan think, to salvage by transplantation the DNA of the embryo-to-be-destroyed, little would be lost other than easily replaceable cellular components (cytoplasm, mitochondria).[7] And so, they find it "difficult to imagine those who favor just war opposing a war against such suffering given the meager loss of a few cellular components" (p. 156).

The McGee/Caplan argument might be summarized thus: "You think of the lives that will be lost because of serious diseases such as Parkinson's—a staggering number of lives—and you thank God for stem cell research." In the face of a structurally similar argument from William Manchester and others, Walzer suggested that the U.S. might have changed its war aims in Japan, and that unconditional surrender should have been an optional goal. McGee and Caplan never even consider analogous possibilities. Only unconditional surrender of Parkinson's disease will do. Slower progress, made possible by research techniques not involving the destruction of embryos, does not seem to be an acceptable aim. "[N]o need is more obvious or compelling than the suffering of half the world at the hand of miserable disease" (p. 155). Progress at relieving this suffering does not seem to be an optional goal. Perhaps McGee and Caplan suppose that we are in something like a moment of supreme emergency. If so, however, they have, at best, made a case for moral necessity—an enemy that must be defeated. They have not even ventured to make a case for strategic necessity—to show that progress cannot be made, even if more slowly, by means that do not involve destruction of embryos. And even the case for moral necessity seems, peculiarly, to commit us to accepting nothing less than the eradication of horrible diseases. Conquer one, and there will be another to be conquered. Supreme emergency becomes a permanent condition, and the "sacrifice" of human lives in service of the common good and the war against suffering never comes to an end. Indeed, knowing that our actions are compelled by "the moral imperative of compassion," we act with a good conscience, bear no burden of criminality, and feel no need to find ways to reinstate the moral code we have overridden.

By comparison with the seriousness of Walzer's analysis of just war theory this attempt at justifying stem cell research seems all too casual. We may contrast it, for example, with a different argument about yet another issue. In a brief piece about euthanasia, written in 1990 when Jack Kevorkian had suddenly garnered attention, William F. May adopted a position on euthanasia that is not unlike Walzer's lengthier argument on the morality of war.[8] Despite judging that the motivations behind the euthanasia movement were "understandable in an age when dying has become such an inhumanly endless business," May offered a number of reasons why acceptance of euthanasia would be bad policy. He argued that "our social policy should allow terminal patients to die but it should not regularize killing for mercy." Even the good end of relieving suffering brought on by "an inhumanly endless" process of dying did not lead May to set aside the ban on euthanasia. But he did recognize something like a moment when both moral and strategic necessity could come together in such a way as to persuade one to override that ban. "I can, to be sure, imagine rare circumstances in which I hope I would have the courage to kill for mercy—when the patient is utterly beyond human care, terminal, and in excruciating pain. . . . On the battlefield I would hope that I would have the courage to kill the sufferer with mercy." Even in such a "moment"—which can scarcely become anything like a "permanent condition"—May seems to think that the ban on killing is not set aside but, rather, overridden, and that a measure of guilt may remain. He writes that "we should not always expect the law to provide us with full protection and coverage for what, in rare circumstances, we may morally need to do. Sometimes the moral life calls us out into a no-man's-land where we cannot expect total security and protection under the law." This is the sort of argument one looks for if a ban is to be overridden.

Did NBAC do better than McGee/Caplan in offering such an argument? To some extent, I believe it did, and, although it will quickly become clear that I think its approach defective, I have considerable respect for the seriousness with which it seems to have proceeded. For example, NBAC declines simply to weigh on some utilitarian balance possible relief of future suffering versus destruction of embryos. This becomes clear in its discussion of Alta Charo's proposal to bypass entirely the issue of the embryo's moral status. Charo suggests that we seek simply to balance deeply felt offense to some (who accept the full humanity of the embryo) over against potentially great health benefits for some future sufferers. "Thus, although it is clear that embryo research would offend some people deeply, she would argue that the potential health benefits for this and future generations outweigh the pain experienced by opponents of the research" (p. 51).

This "Manchesterian" argument eliminates from the outset any possibility of a ban founded upon a belief that certain wrongs ought never be done. NBAC rightly notes that, at least for anyone prepared to contemplate the possibility of a ban on embryo research, this must seem to be sleight of hand. "It might be argued, for example, that placing the lives of embryos in this kind of utilitarian calculus will seem appropriate only to those who presuppose that embryos do not have the status of persons" (p. 51). NBAC does not simply say: "You think of the suffering that will go unrelieved and the lives that will be lost without this research—and you thank God for stem cell research." It at least recognizes the force of the sort of point raised over thirty years ago by Paul Ramsey in a related but somewhat different context:

> I may pause here to raise the question whether a scientist has not an entirely "frivolous conscience" who, faced with the awesome technical possibility that soon human life may be created in the laboratory and then be either terminated or preserved in existence as an experiment, or, who gets up at scientific meet-

ings and gathers to himself newspaper headlines by urging his colleagues to prepare for that scientific accomplishment by giving attention to the "ethical" questions it raises—if he is not at the same time, and in advance, prepared to stop the whole procedure should the "ethical finding" concerning this fact-situation turn out to be, for any serious conscience, murder. It would perhaps be better not to raise the ethical issues, than not to raise them in earnest.[9]

NBAC's conscience is not that frivolous.

Its alternative to such simple utilitarian calculation seems, however, to be a mode of reasoning analogous to what Walzer called a "sliding scale." Its stated aim is "to develop policies that demonstrate respect for all reasonable alternative points of view . . ." (p. 51). To that end, NBAC looks for ways to express "respect" for the embryo, even if not the kind or degree of respect afforded the rest of us. Hence, for example, it offers the following as "a reasonable statement of the kind of agreement that could be possible on this issue": "Research that involves the destruction of embryos remaining after infertility treatments is permissible when there is good reason to believe that this destruction is necessary to develop cures for life-threatening or severely debilitating diseases . . ." (p. 52). That is, the more urgent the cause, the more potential good to be gained from this research, the more respect for the embryo must give way to the research imperative.

That this is a kind of sliding scale becomes clear when we note one of the limits recommended by NBAC. Its report supports research on spare embryos to be discarded after IVF procedures but recommends against creation of embryos solely as research subjects. This is not, however, a line drawn in the sand. It is not a limit that must be respected even if the heavens will fall—or, perhaps, a limit to be overridden only if the heavens really are about to fall. It is, instead, a limit to be chipped away at gradually, as the little words "at this time" in the following sentence indicate: "We do not, at this time, support the federal sponsorship of research involving the creation of embryos solely for research purposes. However, we recognize that in the future, scientific evidence and public support for this type of stem cell research may be sufficient in order to proceed" (p. 55).

This is a kind of "proceed with caution" view. One suspects that the chief "limit" to research discerned by NBAC involves not so much the status of the embryo as the status of "public support."[10] There is no sense here of a limit that could be over-ridden—if at all—only in a moment of supreme emergency, which overriding would involve a burden of criminality, and which limit would somehow have to be reinstated after the fact. Such an argument, if it could be made persuasively, would be a very strong expression of respect for embryos. NBAC does much less, however. From one perspective, in fact, perhaps NBAC's cautious sliding scale shows less respect for embryos than the McGee/Caplan "full speed ahead" approach. One can, as I noted earlier, read McGee/Caplan as justifying stem cell research with a kind of "supreme emergency as a permanent condition" argument. And though I doubt that it really makes sense to posit such a permanent condition of supreme emergency, the attempt does at least acknowledge that nothing less than such extreme circumstances could even claim to justify embryo research. The more judicious, "at this time" approach of NBAC promises, by contrast, a kind of relentless "progress" in what is allowed. It is not really prepared ever to stop. It cannot contemplate or make sense of a ban.

III

Perhaps we can understand, then, why some who reflect upon the morality of stem cell research would not be persuaded by moral reasoning that uses simple utilitarian calculation, applies a "sliding scale," or appeals to "supreme emergency as a perma-nent condition." If we are among the unpersuaded, we are left to contemplate seriously a ban. To do that, however, may compel us to think also about the background beliefs—metaphysical and religious in character—that undergird all our moral reflec-tion. In particular, we will be forced to reflect upon the degree to which relief of suffering has acquired the status of trump in our moral reasoning.

Why might one, even while granting the enormous benefits to be gained from stem cell research, be prepared to contemplate a ban on research that requires the destruction of embryos? How must one think for such a ban to make sense? Clearly, no ban can make sense if we say with McGee and Caplan that "no need is more obvious or compelling than the suffering of half the world at the hand of miserable disease." Nor could any ban make sense in the context of a search, such as NBAC's, for a public policy "consensus" that, while taking objections seriously, will always permit research to proceed. Indeed, despite NBAC's serious attempt to be fair-minded, its understanding of consensus ultimately excludes from consideration precisely those who might be willing to think in terms of a ban.

The very notion of a ban can make sense only if we consider that the fundamental moral question—for a community as for an individual—is *how* we live, not *how long*. If we act simply for the sake of future good, the day will come when those good effects reach an end—which is not a telos, but simply an end. We will have done evil in the present for a future good that does not come to pass.

In his meditations to himself, Marcus Aurelius, the great Stoic emperor of Rome, writes: "Another [prays] thus: How shall I not lose my little son? Thou thus: How shall I not be afraid to lose him?"[11] That is, how shall I not be afraid if the alternative to losing him is doing wrong? In our tradition this emphasis upon how rather than how long we live has been grounded not only in such Stoic thought but also and primarily in Jewish and Christian belief. It has provided the moral background that makes sense of doing justice even if the heavens are about to fall.

One who looks on life this way need not, of course, suppose that beneficence is unimportant or that relief of suffering is of little consequence. Weighty as such values are, however, they have no automatic moral trump. To appreciate this, we can juxtapose passages from two twentieth-century thinkers for whom it was clear that the most important moral question was how we live. In *The Screwtape Letters* C. S. Lewis created a series of letters from a senior devil to a junior tempter—with instructions for tempting a patient, instructions which invert the moral world by inviting us to look at things from the perspective of Satan (for whom God must be "the Enemy"). So, for example, Screwtape advises Wormwood about the attitude toward time which he ought to cultivate in his patient:

> [N]early all vices are rooted in the Future. Gratitude looks to the Past and love to the Present; fear, avarice, lust, and ambition look ahead. . . . [The Enemy] does not want men to give the Future their hearts, to place their treasure in it. We do. . . . [W]e want a man hagridden by the Future—haunted by visions of an imminent heaven or hell upon earth—ready to break the Enemy's commands in the Present if by so doing we make him think he can attain the one or avert the other.[12]

Likewise, reflecting upon "the ethics of genetic control," Paul Ramsey noted the relatively greater importance of an "ethics of means" for religious thinkers.

> Anyone who intends the world as a Christian or as a Jew knows along his pulses that he is not bound *to succeed* in preventing genetic deterioration, any more than he would be bound to retard entropy, or prevent planets from colliding with this earth or the sun from cooling. He is not under the necessity of *ensuring* that those who come after us will be like us, any more than he is bound to *ensure* that there will be those like us to come after us. He knows no such *absolute* command of nature or of nature's God. This does not mean that he will do nothing. But it does mean that as he goes about the urgent business of doing his duty in regard to future generations, he will not begin with the desired *end* and deduce his obligation exclusively from this end. . . . And he will know in advance that any person, or any society or age, expecting ultimate success where ultimate success is not to be reached, is peculiarly apt to devise extreme and morally illegitimate means for getting there.[13]

My aim is not to inject religious beliefs into public discussion of stem cell research. On the contrary, my point is that such beliefs are already there. To see clearly the kind of background beliefs which might make a ban on stem cell research seem reasonable is also to realize that something like a religious vision of the human is at work in arguments *for* such research. Precisely insofar as a ban is not really an option, insofar as proponents of a ban cannot possibly be included in any proposed consensus, the argument for research is that we—human beings—bear ultimate responsibility for overcoming suffering and conquering disease. We know along our pulses that we are, in fact, obligated to succeed, compelled to ensure that future generations not endure suffering which we might have relieved. Possible future benefits so bind our consciences that we are carried along by an argument we might well reject in, say, the ethics of warfare: "You think of the suffering that will go unrelieved and the lives that will be lost without this research—and you thank God for stem cell research."

It is quite true, of course, that a ban on stem cell research requiring destruction of embryos would mean that future sufferers could say to us: "You might have made more rapid progress. You might have helped me." To consider how we should respond to them is to contemplate the moral point of a ban: "Perhaps we could have helped you, but only by pretending that our responsibility to do good is godlike, that it knows no limit. Only by supposing, as modernity has taught us, that suffering has no point other than to be overcome by human will and technical mastery—that compassion means not a readiness to suffer with others but a determination always to oppose suffering as an affront to our humanity. We could have helped you only by destroying in the present the sort of world in which both we and you want to live—a world in which justice is done now, not permanently mortgaged in service of future good. Only, in short, by pretending to be something other than the human beings we are."

Notes

1. An earlier version of this essay was published under the same title in *The Hastings Center Report*, 31 (January–February 2001), pp. 9–16.

2. National Bioethics Advisory Commission, *Ethical Issues in Human Stem Cell Research, Volume I: Report and Recommendations of the National Bioethics Advisory Commission* (September, 1999), p. 69. Future citations of this report will be identified by page number in parentheses within the body of the text.

3. William Manchester, *Goodbye Darkness: A Memoir of the Pacific War* (Boston and Toronto: Little, Brown, 1980), p. 210.

4. Michael Walzer, *Just and Unjust Wars: A Moral Argument with Historical Illustrations* (New York: Basic Books, 1977). Future citations of Walzer will be identified by page number in parentheses within the body of the text.

5. We should note the limits to Walzer's understanding of the supreme emergency faced by Britain: "For the truth is that the supreme emergency passed long before the British bombing reached its crescendo" (p. 261). Long after it was strategically necessary "the raids continued, culminating in the spring of 1945—when the war was virtually won—in a savage attack on the city of Dresden in which something like 100,000 people were killed" (p. 261).

6. Glenn McGee and Arthur Caplan, "The Ethics and Politics of Small Sacrifices in Stem Cell Research," *Kennedy Institute of Ethics Journal*, 9:2 (June 1999), pp. 151–58. Future citations will be identified by page number in parentheses within the body of the text.

7. A puzzling feature of their argument, which I cannot unpack here, has to do with this claim that the trajectory of a human life, which clearly begins with the embryo, is of little importance. As long as certain elements (DNA) are salvaged and given a new trajectory, nothing has been lost. McGee and Caplan develop their claim too briefly for one really to know what its implications are for the matter of personal identity, but, surely, they need to say far more if they are to try to make this move persuasive.

8. William F. May, "Rising to the Occasion of Our Death," *Christian Century*, 107 (July 11–18, 1990), pp. 662f. All citations in the paragraph come from this brief article.

9. Paul Ramsey, *Fabricated Man: The Ethics of Genetic Control* (New Haven and London: Yale University Press, 1970), p. 13.

10. I do not wish to deny the obvious fact that a public commission such as NBAC must pay attention to and measure public support when it makes recommendations. Nevertheless, if one accepts a research ban as one choiceworthy moral option, then one must be open to the possibility that NBAC's responsibility might be to marshal public support for such a ban.

11. Marcus Aurelius, *Meditations*, translated by George Long (South Bend, IN: Regnery-Gateway, 1956), VIII, 31, p. 100.

12. C. S. Lewis, *The Screwtape Letters* (New York: Macmillan, 1973), pp. 69–70.

13. Ramsey, pp. 29–31.

10

Living Life's End[1]

A good bit of public attention in recent years has been focused on developments at the beginning of life: new reproductive technologies, for instance, and research on embryos. But questions about what we ought to do for those near the end of life may be more enduring and are, at least by my lights, more puzzling.

My aim here is to think through a few of those puzzles, not so much to solve them as simply to seek increased clarity about where and why we are puzzled. To the degree that I have a thesis to assert, it is captured nicely in the words of Edgar to Gloucester (*King Lear*, V, ii): "Men must endure / Their going hence, even as their coming hither; / Ripeness is all."

I

Let us suppose that we can agree on the following points. (Not everyone will agree, of course, but the most fruitful clarifications and discussions often arise among those who do already agree on a good bit. Moreover, these points of agreement have been—and, I think, in considerable measure still are—widely shared in our society.)

- We are not "vitalists," as that term is sometimes used. A vitalist thinks that preserving life (even, as it is sometimes put, "mere" biological life) is always the most important human good—and, hence, that life must always be preserved if it can be, at whatever cost to other goods. If we thought this, we could not have a category of permissible "allowing to die."

- We come to our deliberations about end-of-life care with some principles in hand, but we also form judgments about particular cases. There are bound to be instances in which our principles suggest one course of action, while our sense of the particulars of the case inclines us in a different direction. In such instances neither the principles nor our response to the particulars always holds trump in moral reasoning. To be sure, some principles we would be very reluctant to change: they are so fundamental to everything we believe that changing them would be akin to a conversion. Likewise, there are some cases about which we can hardly imagine changing our mind. But our deliberations always move back and forth between principle and particular response, and adjustment can take place on either pole.

- Among the principles we want to uphold but must explore in relation to cases is that we should never aim at or intend the death of any of our fellow human beings (recognizing possible exceptions in cases where they are themselves threatening the lives of others). A slightly different but related formulation would be that we want to affirm the equal dignity of every human being. Hence, we should not think of ourselves as possessors of another's life or judge that another's life is not worthy of our care. (We might add that there is nothing wrong with wishing, hoping, or desiring that a suffering person die; the wrong would lie in acting in a way aimed to bring about that person's death.)

- Committed to such a principle of equal respect, we are led quite naturally to a certain way of caring for others who are ill, suffering, or dying. On the one hand, we should not aim at their death (whether by action or omission). We shouldn't do whatever we do *so that* they will die. On the other hand, because we do not think that continued life is the only good, or necessarily the greatest good, in every circumstance, we are not obligated to do everything that might be done to keep someone alive. If a possible treatment seems useless or (even if useful) quite burdensome for the patient, we are under no obligation to try it or continue it. And in withholding or withdrawing such a treatment, we do not aim at death. We simply aim at another good—the good of life (even if a shorter life) free of the burdens of the proposed treatment. There is nothing terribly unusual about this. All of us, all the time, choose among various life courses open to us. When we are young, we may have many life choices available. The older we get, the more that range narrows. If we become severely ill, the range may be quite narrow indeed. And if we are irretrievably dying, the narrowing process may have left almost no choices at all. Yet, all along the way, we choose a life from among this range of life choices. We may choose a life that is more daring and heroic (though shorter) than some other possibilities. That is not the same as choosing death. Likewise, one might imagine a severely ill patient deciding to forego a painful round of (possibly useful) treatment—choosing thereby a predictably shorter life, but a life free of the burdens of that treatment.

It is quite possible that we can agree on these points, yet not agree entirely on what is right to do in certain cases. Two sorts of cases, in particular, are baffling. There are patients who seem to be increasingly, or even entirely, beyond the reach of our care. The patient in a persistent vegetative state (PVS) would be at the furthest boundary—still clearly a living human being, though seemingly unaware of any care we provide, but able to live indefinitely if given tube feedings. There are also patients to whom care might still be given but who are on a trajectory which can only worsen over time. An example (which I owe to Leon Kass) would be a patient with Alzheimer's disease who has a Stokes-Adams episode (in which a temporary loss of consciousness due to cardiac arrhythmia occurs). One might implant a pacemaker in such a patient, thereby preventing further such episodes, but thereby also making time for further stages of decline from Alzheimer's.

These cases may baffle us, even against the background of agreement I sketched above. In the instance of the PVS patient we may—to put it crassly—wonder what the point is of feeding. In the case of the patient with Stokes-Adams syndrome we may wonder whether we should help them now, knowing that by making cardiac arrest less likely we thereby keep them alive for still greater deterioration from dementia. We can take these two sorts of cases in order and think them through.

II

With regard to a patient in a persistent vegetative state, what is the point of providing care that seems to make no difference to the one who receives it? This is a question any of us might ask ourselves. Rather than addressing it directly, I want to trace briefly some reflections—and a change of mind—that Paul Ramsey wrote of years ago. Writing before a clear distinction had been made between comatose and PVS patients, Ramsey discussed patients in what he called "deep and irreversible coma." We can simplify matters by taking his discussion to refer to PVS patients—which is, I think, more or less the sort of case he had in mind.

In 1970 Ramsey published *The Patient as Person*. Chapter 3, titled "On (Only) Caring for the Dying," is one of the classic early pieces of bioethical writing in this country. Any reader of the chapter will see that (while he is aware of the possibility of "undertreatment") Ramsey's chief concern is "overtreatment." In the course of his discussion Ramsey argues that one basic imperative—"never abandon care"—should govern our treatment decisions. He recognizes that we could effectively abandon proper care for patients by aiming at their death (by action or omission)—but also by providing treatments which for them are either useless or excessively burdensome. If we withdraw or withhold treatment, and do so properly, we are not abandoning care for the person; rather, we are caring in what is now the appropriate manner. So we should never aim at a patient's death, never treat him in a way intended to get him to go away, but we might well give care that provides for him a life free of the burdens of treatment, even if somewhat shorter than possible.

Having worked the argument to this point, Ramsey then considered (in the final section of chapter 3) "two possible qualifications of our duty always to care for the dying." Of the first of these—patients who are "irretrievably inaccessible to human care"—Ramsey was not only asking whether it would be permissible to withdraw treatment from such patients. Because he was clear that one might aim at a patient's death by withholding treatment, the "qualification" he was exploring was whether taking action to kill the patient—to whom it no longer seems to make any difference—might be permissible.

In considering such an exception, Ramsey did not suppose that he was setting aside the principle never to abandon care. On the contrary, his point was that one might argue that care cannot be given to a person who is "beyond" receiving it. And he made the point specifically with reference to feeding.

> The proposed justifiable exception depends on the patient's physiological condition which may have placed him utterly beyond reach. If he feels no suffering, he would feel no hunger if nourishment is withheld. He may be alone, but he can feel no presence. If this is a true account of some comatose patients, then in this sort of case we have correctly located the point at which the crucial moral difference between omission and commission as a guide to faithful actions has utterly vanished. The condition of the patient renders it for him a matter of complete indifference whether humankind's final act toward him directly or indirectly allows death to come. He already is beyond our love and care.

Less than a decade later Ramsey returned to the question of possible qualifications of the duty never to abandon care. In *Ethics at the Edges of Life* he took up again—though with greater care and precision—the question of possible exceptions. He more or less withdrew the earlier exceptions he had proposed, writing that he had ample reason to regret that he had not eliminated them from the manuscript of the earlier book.

Why the change of mind? A full account would draw us into a number of complexities, but a relatively simple answer is that he was no longer certain we can say with confidence when another living human being is beyond the reach of our care. Persuaded in considerable measure by objections Hans Jonas ("a person to me of exemplary moral wisdom") had raised, Ramsey drew back. "The serious objection to searching for such exceptions is that—even within the stringent limits of indications of a patient's impenetrable solitude silencing any need on our parts to feel an obligation to continue to extend care—one might still do the deadly deed to someone . . . who while beyond showing response to us may still be within reach of violation at our hands, and so not altogether in God's keeping."

That sentence ends a paragraph. The next paragraph begins: "But then the objectors shifted, and the objection changed . . . in support of outlooks in medical ethics I never thought of espousing." From Ramsey's attempt to see whether there were any exceptions to the principle which forbade abandoning care (because the agent could no longer give what could not be received), or from the view, "which was never in doubt," that it would be right to let die those who were clearly dying, others moved to a search for reasons for "letting patients die who are in fact not dying."

Which brings us back to the case of the patient in a persistent vegetative state. If at any point it seems that the patient's body is shutting down, that he is going to die quite soon regardless of whether he is given high-caloric feedings, surely we can discontinue feeding without abandoning him in his dying or aiming at his death.

But suppose a different case, in which a patient might live for a decade if fed. Such a patient is certainly severely disabled, but it would be counterintuitive to call him a "dying" patient. He is not irretrievably dying, perhaps not even terminally ill. And if he is not dying, it will be difficult to characterize a decision to stop feeding as simply "letting" or "allowing" this person to die. As Ramsey wrote, try "withholding the *intention to cause* the death of a patient" when acting thus. (This makes feeding quite different from decisions about removing a respirator. One does not know for certain that a patient will be unable to breathe on his own, and, unless we intend to suffocate him if he does breathe successfully on his own, it is possible to remove the respirator while withholding an intention to bring about the person's death.)

We can, of course, readily understand why someone—any of us—might feel that it was useless or made no sense to continue feeding such a person; yet perhaps this is an impulse we should resist. As Hans Jonas put it, we should not "deny the extracerebral body its essential share in the identity of the person." Hence, the body of such a human being, which "still breathes, pulses and functions otherwise, must still be considered a residual continuance of the subject that loved and was loved"—and for whom, therefore, we should never abandon care.

We might worry, of course, that we were now committed to any and all medical interventions which the PVS patient might need in his continuing life. Would we provide all sorts of treatments, even quite invasive ones? And if not, why not? And if we would not provide various invasive treatments, does that mean we should rethink a decision to feed the patient?

The questions and permutations here become endless, of course, and many of them can scarcely be answered in advance. I would be reluctant to withhold antiobiotics for treating a simple infection in such a patient, for it seems to me that I would withhold them only *so that* the patient would die. I'm also confident, however, that I would not think such a patient should have bypass surgery or have a leg amputated. Why the difference?

I think perhaps—trying, as we are, to articulate reasons for what amounts to an intuition—that more invasive treatments seem to make the patient a mere object. I realize, of course, that such persons may seem to be precisely that. Yet I suspect that when we feed this patient we do not so much treat him as an object as try to honor the way in which his (seemingly now) "extracerebral body" retains "its essential share in the identity of the person." It would be harder to think that way when we amputated a leg. Moreover, we could withhold the more invasive interventions while simultaneously withholding an intention that the patient die. But it is hard to believe we could withhold feeding while simultaneously withholding the intention that the patient die.

We can, therefore—or, at least, I think we can—develop what it means never to abandon care of such patients without supposing that we are or must somehow be committed to using every intervention made possible by medical advance. And surely we can do so while acknowledging our mortality and recognizing that it is appropriate to let a dying person die.

III

But the fear that medical advance simply keeps us alive to suffer greater and longer deterioration is a strong one, and it is best discussed by turning to the second sort of case—in which intervening to benefit and preserve life means keeping a person alive for what may well be a long period of deterioration and a yet worse death.

Suppose a person suffering from dementia experiences a Stokes-Adams episode. Why would we not implant a pacemaker in order to prevent further episodes? Almost certainly we would provide a pacemaker if the person were not demented, so why exactly would the presence of dementia make us do otherwise?

One reason we might be tempted not to provide a pacemaker for a demented patient has to do with a certain revulsion some may feel for a life (in particular, our own life or that of a loved one) that has descended deeply into dementia. Even if that demented person is actually quite content, as might well be the case, we may still draw back in the presence or at the thought of that "extracerebral still living body." But if we experience such revulsion, we should struggle against it, however naturally it comes to us—for if we decide against the pacemaker when moved by such feelings, it becomes hard to deny that we are doing this *so that* the demented person will die.

One might reject that conclusion, however, or at least argue with it. The argument would go something like this: In withholding the pacemaker we are not aiming at this person's death. On the contrary, when all of us choose constantly from among the various lives available to us, we are choosing not only a life but also certain possible deaths. We are choosing among the various deaths open to us, making some far more likely than others—but this does not amount to aiming at or intending death. So we might decline the pacemaker for a demented loved one, choosing thereby a likely death from cardiac arrest rather than a death from other causes at the end of a long period of dementia.

This is a serious response, though I do not find it persuasive. Its flaw is that it is grounded less in a desire to benefit the life the patient has than to ask whether continued life would be a benefit. Or we could say that its flaw is that it seeks less to benefit the life the patient has than to manage, shape, and orchestrate the time and circumstances of death. This gets the focus somewhat wrong. After all, the patient we have described with Stokes-Adams syndrome is not necessarily going to die at once if we decline the pacemaker for him. He may live on for some time, suffering occasional episodes, increasingly weak and listless. Hence, for as long as he lives on, our decision deprives him of benefits well within our power to provide without burdening him greatly. Thus, our desire to orchestrate the circumstances of death, to see that he dies from cardiac problems rather than as the end result of a decade of dementia, deflects our focus from helping him to live better for as long as he lives.

Moreover, the desire or attempt to manage and orchestrate the timing and circumstances of death may miss something important about what it means to be human and may, in fact, be poor preparation for death (our own or another's) when it does come. Death means, after all, the defeat of our desire to manage and shape the circumstances of our life. Trying to orchestrate the circumstances of death has the look, therefore, of one last attempt to be what we are not—the author of the story of our life or the life of another. As Daniel Callahan, who would certainly not agree entirely with the direction I am taking, has noted: "However much we work to control the circumstances of our dying, its essence is the loss of ultimate control, the final disenfranchisement of the controlling self."

IV

We are driven back, in short, to one of the central truths about human nature, a truth that complicates matters time and again in bioethics. On the one hand, we fail to do justice to the freedom that characterizes our nature if we suppose that human beings should simply suffer death as the other animals do, untouched by human art. On the other hand, we fail to honor the finitude that (just as much as freedom) characterizes our nature if we try to avoid or escape the trajectory that bodily life takes. "Men must endure / Their going hence, even as their coming hither; / Ripeness is all." The same desire to honor and respect bodily life that inclines us to hesitate before the possibility of engineering the "coming hither" of the next generation should also incline us to hesitate to engineer our "going hence." Euthanasia is the ultimate attempt at managing death (and misses the irony that we are attempting to master the very event that announces our lack of mastery). We are exploring now whether some treatment decisions approach too closely that same managerial attitude, whether they begin to choose death rather than life.

Consider another sort of case: Suppose a diabetic and insulin-dependent person is told by his physician that he has a form of cancer which will almost surely kill him within two years. He is terminally ill, though hardly at this point irretrievably dying. We can suppose also that he accepts the broad moral contours I outlined at the beginning and would not, therefore, think it right to take a drug overdose now in order to avoid what lies ahead. But there is another possible route to such avoidance. He could simply stop taking his insulin, drift off into a diabetic coma, and in this manner orchestrate to some extent the manner of his "going hence."

Why not? Why not shape the circumstances of his dying in this way—seizing upon the fact of his insulin-dependence, just as one might seize upon the fact of a cardiac arrhythmia to avoid years of dementia? Why do we sense, as I certainly do, that giving up his insulin at this point would be choosing death rather than simply choosing a life shorter than some possible lives he might choose?

One thing we might note is that the range of his life choices, though narrowing, remains considerable at this point. He could still decide to run the risks of learning to parachute from an airplane. He could still travel across the country to see a grandchild. He could still go to Florida to watch the baseball teams in spring training. Perhaps doing any of these things would sap his body's energy and result in a somewhat earlier death than would otherwise have occurred, but they would all be choices of life, not death. It is much harder, however, to describe a decision to dispense with his insulin as a choice of a certain kind of life. It would be hard to withhold the insulin at this point while (to use Ramsey's formulation) simultaneously withholding the intention to bring about death.

I can also imagine, however, that a time might come (say, twenty-two months later) when this same person goes into the hospital for what he, his family, and his doctors know will be the last time. No longer simply terminally ill, he is now irretrievably dying. The range of his life choices has narrowed greatly—indeed, is almost nil. If now he makes decisions which shape or orchestrate his manner of dying, he does so in a context where he is not choosing or aiming at death—an intention that would, after all, suggest an absurdly inflated sense of the possibilities still open to him. I would think that deciding to say goodbye, to stop taking the insulin, and to drift off into a diabetic coma would no longer amount to aiming at or choosing death. He would be shaping—even, if we wish, engineering—the manner of his dying, but not in what seems an unacceptable way.

This is as far as I can press my own reflections on these matters, but the central question is, I hope, clear. Take any case of a person who no longer seems to have much of a life. (I put it this way to capture not how we ought to think but how we often feel.) And suppose this person may die somewhat sooner if not treated but may live an indefinite period of time (in this less than desirable condition) if treated. And suppose, finally, that the treatment itself is not painful, is not unusually costly, does not require great inconvenience for the person being treated, and is not so invasive as to seem to make of the person a mere object. The treatment will benefit the life he has, even though one might be tempted to say that it's not much of a benefit to have that life. If we withhold treatment in such a case, would we simply be shaping or orchestrating the manner of death in a morally acceptable way? Or would it be more accurate and honest to say that withholding treatment in these circumstances would be not merely shaping the manner of dying but choosing and aiming at death—withholding treatment in the hope that he will die as a result?

Whatever our uncertainties, and however precisely we respond to such cases, we need to do so in a way that attempts to hold on to the truth of our human condition. We should not want to think of ourselves as the author of the story of our own life or that of another—nor, therefore, as one who exercises ultimate *author*ity over life. Indeed, when we think that way, or to the degree we think that way, we will almost certainly be unable to come to terms with the fact of death, and our attempt to deal with it is bound to be distorted. Some shaping and orchestrating of living and dying we all must do. But it is a true depiction of our humanity to say that "Men must endure / their going hence, even as their coming hither." As Gene Outka put it in a somewhat different context, with respect to every person whose life is given us to care for, we are "enjoined to honor from first to last the space he occupies and the time he has.

Note

1. An earlier version of this essay was published under the same title in *First Things*, no. 153 (May 2005), pp. 17–21.

11

Why Remember?[1]

In the movie *Memento* (released in 2001) the central character, Leonard Shelby, sustains a blow to the head from an intruder who has already raped and killed Shelby's wife. The movie tells the story of Shelby's search to find and kill that intruder, but his search is enormously complicated by his "condition," as he calls it. The blow to the head has left him unable to form any new memories. If he discovers a clue, he will not remember it a few minutes later. He resorts to taking Polaroid snapshots of people and writing himself notes about them on the back of the picture. He tattoos reminders on his body. He learns to bluff, pretending to recognize people who look at him as if he should know them. He is aware that others might trick him, might use him for their own purposes, might even get him to kill someone whom they wanted out of the way. And, in fact, that is precisely what happens in the movie.

The irony is that even were Leonard to succeed in avenging the death of his wife, he would not remember it. And, hence, he is locked into a never-ending search, always with a sense of desperation as he attempts to find ways to remind himself of relevant details. The movie's tale is told in a way impossible to summarize—beginning, so to speak, from the end and moving step by step back to the time when Leonard was first injured. The viewer is constantly puzzled, therefore, because the viewer never knows more than Leonard does. We experience just a little of what it would be like to try to make sense of our world if we lacked the capacity to form new memories and connect them with older ones. Every morning Leonard wakes up knowing that his wife is dead, but entirely unable to remember how long this has been true. And at certain moments we sense both the pathos and the desperation of a life that simply cannot organize events coherently because everything is always new. "How am I supposed to heal if I can't feel time?" Leonard asks.

To watch *Memento* is to be drawn into reflection about the place of memory in our sense of self and in the construction of a meaningful life. The more we enter into Leonard's desperation, the more apparent it becomes that memory is central to our understanding of what it means to live as a human being. There are mysteries here well worth pondering, even if we cannot get to the bottom of them.

I

In its October 2002 meeting the President's Council on Bioethics heard from two experts in memory research (James McGaugh and Daniel Schachter) about current research into the formation of memory, into attempts to enhance memory, and into the possibility of blocking the formation of long-term "explicit" memory of certain events. (Explicit memory may be contrasted with implicit memory, which is the retention of certain skills, such as "how" to ride a bicycle. Explicit memory is the memory of "what," of events. Thus, Dr. McGaugh noted that it might be possible for a person suffering from Alzheimer's to remember the mechanics of playing golf while being unable to remember how many strokes he had taken on any hole.) For now, at least, it appears that we are more able to block memory than to enhance it, and we can imagine that such erasure of memory might be very appealing in certain traumatic circumstances.

Anti-anxiety drugs or beta-blockers can be used to prevent the formation of long-term memories. This is possible because, in the formation and consolidation of those memories, our emotions play a significant role. For example, the rush of adrenaline during intense emotional experience may help to form especially powerful memories. Because that is true, we can understand why a beta-blocker, which counteracts the effects of adrenaline, might, if administered immediately after a highly emotional experience, diminish the strength of our memory of the event.

We can imagine persons in a range of circumstances who might experience severe trauma and be likely to suffer post-traumatic stress disorder (PTSD)—those who've witnessed a horrible accident, soldiers in battle, a woman who has been raped, rescue workers at a disaster, a child who has seen his mother killed (or, perhaps, just, who has seen his mother die). If such people were administered beta-blockers soon after the event and for several weeks thereafter, they would (as Dr. Mc-Gaugh put it in conversation with the council) experience "a significant decrease in the expression of PTSD" months later. Why should they suffer such painful memories if the means to relieve them are at hand?

Clearly, the question is actually more complicated than I have thus far made it seem. We do not want to remember everything that happens in life, and we need to be able to forget a lot. To take a striking literary example, Dr. Watson was astonished to realize that the same Sherlock Holmes who had written a technical monograph distinguishing 140 different forms of cigar, cigarette, and pipe tobacco (and the differences in their ash) was entirely ignorant of the Copernican Theory and the bodies of our solar system.

> "You appear to be astonished," he [Holmes] said, smiling at my [Watson's] expression of surprise. "Now that I do know it I shall do my best to forget it."
>
> "To forget it!"
>
> "You see," he explained, "I consider that a man's brain originally is like a little empty attic, and you have to stock it with such furniture as you choose. A fool takes in all the lumber of every sort that he comes across, so that the knowledge which might be useful to him gets crowded out, or at best is jumbled up with a lot of other things, so that he has a difficulty in laying his hands upon it. Now the skilful workman is very careful indeed as to

what he takes into his brain-attic. He will have nothing but the tools which may help him in doing his work, but of these he has a large assortment, and all in the most perfect order. . . ."

"But the Solar System!" I protested.

"What the deuce is it to me?" he interrupted impatiently: "you say that we go round the sun. If we went round the moon it would not make a pennyworth of difference to me or to my work."

Whatever we may think of Holmes's qualifications as a scientist of the brain or his judgment of what is likely to be useful to him in his work, he is right to see that we must forget a great deal if we are to live at all effectively and efficiently—though, as we shall see, such a pronounced, "Holmesian," sense of mastery over what one forgets and remembers may be less fitting for human beings than a more humble sense of organizing, reorganizing, and giving new meaning. But it is clear that the memory must sort and organize experience for us, not just retain an unorganized collection of events. Why not, then, as an aspect of this sorting activity, take steps that are within our power to keep our lives from being crippled or burdened by painful memories?

There could, of course, be complications that would have to be considered in any plan to block memory formation. Criminal prosecutions of those guilty of heinous deeds might depend precisely on *not* blocking the memory of their victims or of witnesses, on retaining as clear and precise a recollection as possible. Or, to take a very different sort of complication, suppose it were possible to keep soldiers from remembering the horrors of battle—so that they experienced no interval of hesitation at the thought of combat. That might make them more efficient and effective killers, but would we really think it desirable?

Nevertheless, we can think of instances that might tempt us and might, at first, seem relatively free of complication. Imagine rescue workers sent in to search for those trapped in the rubble of the World Trade Center after the attack of September 11, likely to carry with them forever horrible memories of the dead and the maimed. They could start on beta-blockers immediately after emerging from the rubble and perhaps be spared. Or a woman who had seen her young child murdered could likewise immediately begin medication, lest the rest of her life should be consumed by such painful memories.

Even in such cases there are complications that might still trouble us. Granting that these people could consent to take the medication, how could they know or decide in that moment whether doing so was wise? Is that the moment in which to decide whether one wants to carry such painful memories along throughout life or to erase them? Perhaps we could argue that rescue workers, knowing that they might at any time find themselves in such tragic circumstances, might think the matter through in advance and, as it were, give advance authorization to be so treated after the fact. But can one actually think this through knowledgeably in advance of the experience? And, more important still, if a life is essentially a narrative, we have to ask how we want to think of ourselves in relation to that narrative. Am I simply the author of my story—picking and choosing what is to be included in the remembered, organized account? Or is my authorship a more limited one—finding ways to make do, to fit even traumatic experiences into the overall story and thereby make sense of it? Exaggerating our own authorship ignores important characteristics of the story of a life. It ignores, for example, the fact that the first years of our life become part of our own memory largely through the shared memories of others. It ignores the fact that one's life exists not only in the privacy of one's own memory but also in the stories others tell about us. Perhaps, therefore, a certain modesty is in order when we think of constructing the story of our life. Even were we able to deal with painful memories by erasing them, it might still be better to struggle—with the help of others—to fit them into a coherent story that is the narrative of our life.

II

Even granting that, however, we might still wonder whether it would be wrong to block painful memories. Do we have some kind of obligation to remember? If so, to whom would such a duty be owed? I suspect we can imagine circumstances in which we might think that there is indeed an obligation not to forget. For the sake of victims treated unjustly we may need to remember the evil done them, and, in fact, this might be necessary not just for the sake of the victims themselves but for our common humanity. Not to remember the face of evil is to miss the evil of which we ourselves are capable. Not to remember evils done to others is to make it impossible for us to tell the stories of their lives fully and truthfully, which is required not for the sake of vengeance but for the sake of justice. (This is especially true when we remember that the story of one's life is not only one's private creation but is dependent also on the memories of others and the stories they tell.)

Quite often, to be sure, there may be no easy or foolproof way to integrate painful memories into the ongoing story of one's life. We may need help to manage such a task. It may call for imagination, radical rethinking of who we are, the search for a new direction that can, at least to some extent, redeem the past by taking it up into a way of life that gives it new meaning. Thus, for example, in 1957, the son of Hermann Goering entered a cloistered monastery. "He had done so, as I recall," David Novak writes,

> because he could not live in the world any other way consider-
> ing his name and his family heritage. This news report touched
> me deeply because so much of our being-in-the-world is not
> our own decision. We begin to discover in late adolescence the
> limits of our own existence and, concurrently, the moral pos-
> sibilities for us within these limits. Hermann Goering's son did
> not choose to be Hermann Goering's son; he did not choose to
> be born a German in the 1930s. What he did choose, however,
> was to make his own life in a place where everyone assumes a
> new name, in a place not of Germany or even of this world.

There is something deeply humane about such a decision. Goering's son did not, of course, have the option of simply forgetting the painful truth of who he was, but, had he been able to do so, I suspect that it would have diminished rather than enhanced his person.

Human life has a narrative quality, and, in Stephen Crites's felicitous phrase, each present moment is a "tensed" present. It stretches out in two directions—incorporating the past and reaching out toward the future. Each moment, therefore, contains a narrative in miniature, and every life is a story whose plot may be partially hidden in the present. We cannot know the full significance of any moment in that story—what it contributes and how it affects other moments—unless and until we can read the story as a whole. If we cannot know the full meaning of any moment in a life apart from its place in the entire narrative of that life, our task is not so much to erase embarrassing, troubling, or painful moments, but, as best we can and with whatever help we are given, to attempt to redeem those moments by drawing them into a life whose whole transforms and transfigures them.

III

Perhaps, therefore, the issue is not so much whether we have an obligation to remember—though there is something to that—but whether the erasure of painful memories does not diminish our humanity. "Remember," the ancient Israelites are commanded by their Lord, "remember that you were a slave in the land of Egypt, and the LORD your God redeemed you." Even the memory of their bondage is not to be erased, but, rather, drawn into a story that, by God's power and grace, is transformed into one of redemption. To be sure, the Hebrew prophets sometimes describe this God's forgiveness of Israel's sin as "not remembering." Perhaps that is fitting for God, or perhaps the metaphor ought not be pressed. But, in any case, when the prophet Ezekiel describes the restored and reconstituted Israel—in which, presumably, God will no longer remember Israel's sin—Israel's own task is described quite differently. "Then you will remember your evil ways, and your deeds that were not good." Human beings, at any rate, are not to erase the memories that give them pain but to place those memories into a new, larger, and redemptive story.

This is appropriate, at least in part, because genuinely human life has an embodied (and therefore limited) character to which we should be faithful. If we consider the facts recounted earlier about how we might prevent painful memories from forming, we are, in fact, reminded that we are bodies. The beta-blockers or anti-anxiety drugs that block formation of long-term memories are drugs that work on the body in countless ways. They do more than prevent the formation and consolidation of memory. Or, perhaps better, we should say that they do that precisely because they affect other aspects of our bodily life—in particular, the emotions. It is not fitting, therefore, that we should construct the narrative of our life in a way that largely bypasses its embodied character.

In the famous sixth book of the *Aeneid*, Aeneas travels to the underworld in search of his father, Anchises. He finds him "deep in the lush green of a valley"—in Elysium, where the souls of the blessed are. Most of these souls, however, are not destined to remain there indefinitely. Rather, most are to be reincarnated in the bodies of human beings—a fact which, in the poem, provides Anchises the opportunity to survey for Aeneas the future generations of Romans who will be his descendants. When Aeneas inquires how this will take place, Anchises points to the river Lethe, around which many of the souls are gathered.

> Souls for whom
> A second body is in store: their drink
> Is water of Lethe, and it frees from care
> In long forgetfulness.

These souls, Anchises tells Aeneas, will drink of Lethe "[t]hat there unmemoried they may see again / The heavens and wish re-entry into bodies." Having lost all memory of their former life, these souls will now be given entirely new identities. It is not that a previous identity will undergo transformation by being taken up into what is new and thereby reconfigured; rather, it is that these selves, since they are not essentially bodies at all, can be "unmemoried" without any sense of loss. Their memories are no part of who they truly are, because their bodies are not. Perhaps this makes good sense if we think the body accidental to the meaning and nature of a human life, but if, on the contrary, we do not merely *inhabit* but *are* our bodies, to be "unmemoried" would be to become either more or less than human. Unless we think of ourselves as gods, the more likely result is clear.

How essential memory is to our sense of what it means to have a human life may be seen if we consider a life "story" that—almost—is no longer a story, because, lacking memory, it lacks coherence, lacks connection, lacks a story line. In a chapter titled "The Lost Mariner," Oliver Sacks has described the life of such a person—Jimmie G., who suffered from severe retrograde amnesia. (Jimmie's condition, though not caused by an injury, is not unlike that of Leonard Shelby in *Memento*. It is a similar story of one who is essentially "lost" in the world, though Jimmie, of course, has not embarked on any mission of vengeance.) Jimmie had served, and served competently, in the navy until the time of his discharge in 1965. It was in 1975 that he was admitted to a home in which he came under the care of Dr. Sacks. Yet he could remember almost nothing after the year 1945.

Jimmie had been drafted in 1943 at age 17 and had served as a radio operator on a submarine. He could remember clearly the end of the war and could recount his plans for the future at the time the war ended, but that was as far as his memory went; 1945 was still his "present." He could recall the town where he grew up and his school days; he could name the submarines on which he had served; he remained fluent in Morse code; he was good at solving puzzles (so long as they could be done relatively quickly). But his memory stopped at 1945, and he thought of himself as nineteen years old.

This was, however, by no means the most devastating result of his illness. Far more aw(e)ful was the fact that he could form no new memories that would last more than a few seconds. David Hume famously claimed that human beings are no more than collections or bundles of sensations. In Jimmie, Sacks notes, one sees what such a "Humean" person would actually be like—"every sentence uttered being forgotten as soon as it is said, everything forgotten within a few minutes of being seen." Jimmie's problem seems to have been precisely the inability to form long-term memories, to consolidate short-term memory into anything lasting. That is to say, his problem was a pronounced and extended version of what we might deliberately bring about in much more limited and defined circumstances if we were to administer beta-blockers to rescue workers emerging from the rubble. "It was not, apparently, that he failed to register in memory, but that the memory traces were fugitive in the extreme, and were apt to be effaced within a minute, often less. . . ."

We can ponder the meaning for human life of memory loss—
or erasure—if we take note of Jimmie's inability to make the
events of his life "connect." He has many moments of experience, of course, but each is new. Each is, in the strictest sense of
the word, moment-ary. Hence—and does this not seem to be
crucial?—one cannot discuss Jimmie's condition with him. "If a
man has lost a leg or an eye, he knows he has lost a leg or an eye;
but if he has lost a self—himself—he cannot know it, because he
is no longer there to know it." We might imagine—on a smaller
and less destructive scale, to be sure—a world in which some of
us, sometimes, blocked the formation of painful memories and
therefore did not fully share a past, could not fully connect, with
others whose memory of those events was intact. How could
we live truthfully, or confidently, in such a world?

IV

If to have a human life is, at least in part, to have a life story in
progress, then Jimmie has a life largely in the memories of others.
It is by no means unimportant that they should so honor his shared
humanity that they, so to speak, continually sustain and construct
the narrative of his life, but his loss remains great. Each of us is constantly active in memory, constructing and reconstructing the story
of his life or her life. We forget some things, of course, as we must.
And over time we give new and different significance to events
we might once have thought fixed in their meaning; they take on
a new shape as the overall shape of life changes. But to construct
the narrative of one's life not through thought and conversation,
struggle and prayer, but simply by erasing some of the materials
of that life is to risk losing what is essential to being human. If we
cannot say who we have been, we can never know who we are.
Our humanity lies not in mastery over the construction of our
life story but in the virtues by which we accept the limits of the
body, live truthfully in the face of the past, and seek to give new
meaning to what is painful or misguided in that past.
   It is true, of course, that the more painful the memory, the more
difficult it may be to believe that anything in the future could

transfigure it or could draw it into a life story that we could bear to acknowledge as our own—and the more tempted, therefore, we may be to seek a technological fix. At the very end of the story of Job, in its canonical version, the Lord restores Job's fortune—indeed, his material and familial blessings become even greater than they were before his trials. Scholars, of course, often characterize this prose epilogue as an addendum to the poem that tells Job's story—an addendum that drastically alters the story's meaning. Instead of a poem in which Job simply suffers inexplicably, we are given—with the epilogue—a story in which Job's suffering is finally redeemed and given coherent meaning.

Many—unable or unwilling to suppose that Job's sufferings might be in any sense redeemed—are likely to prefer the poem without the epilogue. They will prefer Archibald MacLeish's *J. B.*, in which, without any claims for redemptive meaning, one simply bears what comes with human dignity.

> The candles in churches are out.
> The lights have gone out in the sky.
> Blow on the coal of the heart
> And we'll see, by and by.

But note that neither reading—neither a reading which encourages us to hope that what is painful in the past may be transfigured and given new, redemptive meaning, nor a reading which encourages us to bear the ills of life with human dignity, finding in them occasions for courage, endurance, and mutual support—neither of these readings supposes that simply erasing the painful past takes seriously the narrative quality of human life.

"How great, my God, is this force of memory, how exceedingly great! It is like a vast and boundless subterranean shrine. Who has ever reached the bottom of it? Yet this is a faculty of my mind and belongs to my nature; nor can I myself grasp all that I am." Thus, St. Augustine, in one of the most famous discussions of memory ever written. Dive as deep as we may into that "subterranean shrine," into the depths of the memories that constitute the story of our life, and we cannot yet see the full meaning of any of life's events. Caught as we are in the midst of the story, doing our best to follow a plot whose twists and turns we may not entirely fathom, we cannot see anything from the perspective of the end of the story—and, therefore, cannot say fully who we are or what the events of our life may mean.

That is the gist of Augustine's "confession": that because only God can catch the heart and hold it still, because we cannot attain that authorial perspective on the end (and, therefore, the full meaning) of our life, God knows us better than we know ourselves. Quite a different spirit is expressed in the famous claim made by Rousseau at the outset of his *Confessions:*

> Let the last trump sound when it will, I shall come forward with this work in my hand, to present myself before my Sovereign Judge, and proclaim aloud: ". . . I have bared my secret soul as Thou thyself hast seen it, Eternal Being."

One who supposed that he could attain that godlike perspective on the meaning of his life might perhaps be in a position to know what experiences were so painful that they were better obliterated from memory. If, on the contrary, we know ourselves as bodies who live in time, whose lives must have a narrative quality but who cannot know the end or full meaning of our life story, then our task is not to erase memory but to connect and integrate memories—to live the story as best one can who does not yet know how the plot will work out. Perhaps, in so doing, some of us will believe that there is no past so painful that it cannot be transfigured and redeemed in a truthful story. Perhaps, in so doing, others among us may suspect that the best we can do is blow on the coal of the heart and see by and by (how the plot takes its course). But neither approach will find good reason to act as if we already knew the full meaning of life's story. In either case we are led to acknowledge our limits, to honor the narrative quality of human life, to accept our need to sustain the life stories of one another, and to wonder at the mysterious depths of a "memoried" human life.

Notes

1. An earlier version of this essay appeared under the same title in *First Things*, no. 135 (August/September 2003), pp. 20–24.

Index